TRAVEL
WITHIN

The 7 Steps
to Wisdom
and Inner Peace

First published by O Books, 2008
O Books is an imprint of John Hunt Publishing
Ltd., The Bothy, Deershot Lodge, Park Lane,
Ropley, Hants, SO24 0BE, UK
office1@o-books.net
www.o-books.net

Distribution in:

UK and Europe
Orca Book Services
orders@orcabookservices.co.uk
Tel: 01202 665432 Fax: 01202 666219 Int. code
(44)

USA and Canada
NBN
custserv@nbnbooks.com
Tel: 1 800 462 6420 Fax: 1 800 338 4550

Australia and New Zealand
Brumby Books
sales@brumbybooks.com.au
Tel: 61 3 9761 5535 Fax: 61 3 9761 7095

Far East (offices in Singapore, Thailand, Hong
Kong, Taiwan)
Pansing Distribution Pte Ltd
kemal@pansing.com
Tel: 65 6319 9939 Fax: 65 6462 5761

South Africa
Alternative Books
altbook@peterhyde.co.za
Tel: 021 555 4027 Fax: 021 447 1430

Text copyright Dave Cunningham and
Jamshid Hosseini 2008

Design: Stuart Davies

ISBN: 978 1 84694 133 7

A CIP catalogue record for this book is available
from the British Library.

Printed by Digital Book Print

O Books operates a distinctive and ethical publishing philosophy in
all areas of its business, from its global network of authors to
production and worldwide distribution.
This book is produced on FSC certified stock, within ISO14001
standards. The printer plants sufficient trees each year through
the Woodland Trust to absorb the level of emitted carbon in
its production.

TRAVEL WITHIN

The 7 Steps to Wisdom and Inner Peace

Jamshid Hosseini

with Dave Cunningham

BOOKS

Winchester, UK
Washington, USA

CONTENTS

Preface   vii

Introduction   1

Chapter 1: The End   6
Chapter 2: You Are Everything   11
Chapter 3: No Secret   17
Chapter 4: Wisdom and Inner Peace?   19
Chapter 5: Philosophy   23
Chapter 6: Science   31
Chapter 7: Religion   36
Chapter 8: One Man's Journey   47
Chapter 9: The 7 Steps   56
Chapter 10: Wanting   60
Chapter 11: Receiving   66
Chapter 12: Giving   72
Chapter 13: Balance   80
Chapter 14: Satisfaction   92
Chapter 15: Detachment   98
Chapter 16: Oneness   105
Chapter 17: Truth, Reality and Consciousness   114
Chapter 18: The Living Universe   121
Chapter 19: Your Practical Guide   127
Chapter 20: A Roundtable Discussion   131

Epilogue   159

Works Cited   160

PREFACE

Maybe you're the impatient type who just wants to skip straight to the seven steps: "Why wait until Chapter 9? I can skim all seven steps standing right here in the bookstore (or library) and reach Nirvana before I get to the parking lot."

Not likely. This is not a Get-Spiritually-Rich-Quick book. The masters from whom we learned spent lifetimes in their pursuits of wisdom and inner peace. Instead, think of this book as a road map. You don't glance at a map and instantly become transported to your destination. You still have to make the journey. So we encourage you to spend some time with the first eight chapters so you understand the roots of wisdom.

A NOTE on the dualism of this text: Some of the concepts in this book are mystical, while others are based on research. To present the whole picture, we need to explore both sides of the human brain: the logic of your left hemisphere and the creativity of your right hemisphere. Therefore, some chapters (for example, the sections on science, philosophy and religion) appeal to your ability to reason, while other sections appeal to your ability to dream.

A NOTE on the use of the editorial "we:" While some parts of this book include my personal story, this is not about my journey. It's about yours. Members of the human race have been pursuing transcendental experiences, wisdom and inner peace since before the dawn of the written word. It is our journey, all of us. So, while some instances force me to use the personal "I" because it refers to my own life, I will use the collective "we" whenever possible to emphasize that we're all in this together.

A NOTE on capitalization: In this text, we capitalize certain words that we consider proper nouns: Wanting, Having, Receiving, Balance, Satisfaction, Detachment and Oneness. These are the names of the seven steps to wisdom and inner peace, and we capitalize them to create a distinction between the specific step and the usual context of those words. When we write those words in lower case, it is to indicate their more commonplace usage.

We also capitalize words like "the Absolute" and "the Force" because these are the names of specific entities or conditions, however ethereal they may seem. "Absolute Bliss Consciousness" and other terms for "Oneness" are capitalized because these are states of being that have been quantified and identified by those names and others. If we use "oneness" in lower case, we simply mean a sense of being united into one. Capitalized, "Oneness" is defined in the dictionary as "the experience of the absence of egoic identity boundaries and, according to some traditions, the realization of the awareness of the absolute interconnectedness of all matter and thought in space-time, or one's ultimate identity with God."

INTRODUCTION

John Lennon pleaded with us to imagine there's no heaven ... no countries ... nothing to kill or die for ... no religion ... no possessions ... no need for greed or hunger ... a brotherhood of man, living life in peace.

Were these the words of a silly dreamer, a true prophet, or just a capitalist rock singer? It doesn't matter whether Lennon believed his own imagination or not. Approximately 110 wars are being fought at this very moment all around the world, according to the Carter Center, and almost one-third of them are major armed conflicts with a thousand or more deaths. At least 11 nations possess nuclear weapons or the capability of making them, and more than 30,000 nuclear warheads are pointed in directions all over the planet right now.

Iran may be next to join this mad party. As a native Iranian who knows that culture well, I can tell you that if the Iranian government acquires nuclear capability, it will use it. If the strike comes against the United States, the root reason will be frustration. Few in the Middle East have the freedom and wealth of the West, and they see no way to get it. So the next-best answer is to cut the big guys down to size. Pull them back to our level.

Does this surprise you, that an Iranian would say such things? Did you expect me to preach the glories of Islam and rail against the greed, corruption and hedonism of the West? It's true that western governments have taken many missteps over the last 200 years or more, but I am blessed to have seen through many eyes.

I've been rich and poor, Persian and American, Hindu and Buddhist, alive and dead. I practiced Baha'i Faith in Iran and was beaten by Muslims for it. I begged for my food in India. I lived on a hill overlooking a king's palace in Iran, and I toiled for a monk in Katmandu. I took counsel from the famous Rajneesh in Pune, and I built my own successful business in California. I was nearly killed twice during the Iran-Iraq war, and to conquer fear of death, my master in India asked me to drink cobra venom tea so that I would die. I did it.

But this story is not about me. Ultimately, it is about you. All my journeys began as travels of the physical body, but as wisdom and insight grew, I saw them for what they really were: travels within. And that is something you can do easily, no matter where your life has taken you.

My studies of philosophy, science and religion guided me deep inside, and eventually a realization struck me with such impact, it felt like the most glorious and spectacular red-gold sunrise you could ever imagine: the dream world that John Lennon sang about is real. It exists right now, inside every one of us, buried, perhaps, but there.

In the pages to follow, we will explain why we are convinced of this, and we will endeavor to support it with facts and logic. We will detail these 7 Steps to Wisdom and Inner Peace:

1. Wanting
2. Receiving
3. Giving
4. Balance
5. Satisfaction
6. Detachment
7. Oneness

Through this progression of steps, we have found that fundamental truths govern everything in the universe. An absolute answer for every "Big Question" is available for those who are open to it. And even more amazing was the realization that these answers are so simple.

If this strikes you as religious double-talk, we must pause here to assure you that "Travel Within" is not aligned with any religious doctrine. We believe the concepts in this book will speak to your heart whether you're a Jew, Muslim, Christian, Hindu, Buddhist, Taoist, Scientologist or atheist. The core concepts expressed in the following pages won't conflict with the followers of Moses, Muhammad, Jesus or Lao Tzu. They may challenge you to consider some uncomfortable ideas, especially if your mind is closed, but they won't clash with spirituality, because all spiritual paths lead to the same destination. It's known by different names, but from A to Z, they're really all the same – Avalon, Absolute Bliss Consciousness, Canaan, Elysium, Glory, Happy Hunting Ground, Hawaiki, Heaven, Nirvana, Paradise, Shangri-La, Tir Na Nog, Valhalla, Zion...

We're particularly fond of a different "final destination" term, one found in Zoroastrianism: "House of Good Thinking."

You will not need faith to accept the ideas in this book, but "good thinking" will certainly help. The goal of this text is a lofty one, but perhaps not impossible: to elevate human consciousness enough so that we may avoid the cataclysmic disaster that lies ahead in one of our possible futures. It has been predicted by scientists, politicians, authors, futurists and, of course, most major religions.

The "Doomsday Clock," as estimated by the Bulletin of the Atomic Scientists, stands at seven minutes to midnight, which suggests that nuclear Armageddon is not far off. The good news is that the Doomsday Clock doesn't always tick in the same direction. We can force it backward. For example, in 1953, after the U.S. and Soviet Union both tested thermonuclear devices within a nine-month span, the Doomsday Clock stood at 11:58 p.m., leaving us just two "minutes" from annihilation. In subsequent years, events like the Strategic Arms Limitation Treaty earned us 10 extra "minutes" of breathing room.

The Doomsday Clock was adjusted again in 2002, after the al Qaeda attacks of 9/11/01 and subsequent evidence that terrorist groups were pursuing nuclear and biological weapons. By whatever system of measurement you choose, we are running out of time. Something must change at the fundamental level of human nature if we are to survive.

Shi'ite creed anticipates the return of the 12th Imam, known as the Mahdi, the righteous descendant of the Prophet Muhammad. His return is expected to be preceded by cosmic chaos, war, bloodshed and pestilence. After this cataclysmic confrontation between the forces of good and evil, the Mahdi is supposed to lead the world into an era of universal peace.

Christians tell a similar story in different terms: the Second Coming of Jesus, the End of Time and Judgment Day. Different sects believe different versions. Latter-Day Saints, for example, are convinced that we have already entered our "last days."

Do we really need to find ourselves up to our knees in blood before salvation arrives? And is it really necessary for us to rely on an outside power to save us, like Jesus, Buddha or the 12th Imam?

What if the answer were actually within ourselves? What if the physical and metaphysical paths of inquiry – science and faith – led to the same place? What if God, love, heart, brain, man, woman, animal, vegetable, mineral, matter and void were really all just different expressions of the same force?

You could call that force anything you like – energy, God, the Tao, Allah or, as George Lucas did in his "Star Wars" movies, simply "the Force." We firmly believe this force exists and connects us to everything else in the universe as a common family. We're all parts of the same whole. More importantly, we believe this force is driven by a natural tendency to balance itself. The simplest demonstration of this is the way a spinning object "insists" on becoming a sphere.

Physicists have determined that planets, stars and galaxies form when particles of matter, driven by basic physical forces, naturally coalesce into spinning objects. These objects may start out lumpy and oblong, but the longer they spin, the more balanced they become.

Your perception of the Earth may be one of rugged terrain, tall mountains, deep oceans and vast deserts. Not a perfect sphere by any means, is it? But it's all a matter of perception. If the Earth were shrunk to the size of a billiard ball and placed in your hand, its surface would look as smooth as a real billiard ball. That's how insignificant Mount Everest is, in the grand scheme.

We are spinning toward balance and perfection, both as a planet and as a species. It is our natural tendency. But that doesn't mean we'll reach our destination. Galaxies and solar systems can collide and destroy each other. So can civilizations.

No one will ever write a book capable of stopping an asteroid from smashing into our planet and triggering our extinction. But perhaps someone can write a book that will stop us from smashing into each other and triggering our own extinction.

We must take hope wherever we can find it. If we can build a rocket capable of destroying or diverting a "doomsday asteroid" so it doesn't annihilate us, we must do so. And if we can build peace – personal, inner peace that leads to peace between neighbors, tribes, nations and religions – we must do so.

This book is a recipe for that kind of peace, which we hope will spread throughout the world, one individual at a time. We're not naïve enough to expect that it will happen, but we are naïve enough to believe that it *can* happen.

Inner peace and happiness are closely related, and if the ideas presented in these pages merely lead to greater happiness, they will indeed be useful. America, land of wealth and abundance, is often mistaken for a place of widespread happiness, but less than one in three Americans claims to be happy in their lives. Obviously, the key to happiness lies somewhere beyond material abundance.

My decision to write this book is simply an expression of a species following its natural urge to balance itself. If you read these chapters and achieve greater balance and inner peace in your own life, then the change has begun. And my wish will be fulfilled.

Jamshid Hosseini
Woodland Hills, California

Chapter One

THE END

"It is by going down into the abyss that we recover the treasures of life."
Joseph Campbell

One bite from a king cobra can inject enough pure venom to kill 30 strong men. In India, this snake is both feared and revered. Despite its power to destroy, the cobra is believed to be a legendary protector. Stories tell of how it saved the life of the Buddha and gave protection to the Jain Muni Parshwanath. Cobras were worshiped for their immortality – a belief that probably originated from those who watched the snakes shed their skin and emerge with newborn freshness.

Whether or not you accept its beauty, mystery and supernatural powers, there's no arguing with the fact that a cobra must be respected. Its fangs can inflict cortical blindness, paralysis, respiratory failure and cardiac arrest, all within 30 minutes of a bite. Each year, an estimated 20,000 people in India die from snake bite.

When my spiritual guru asked me to drink a tea-and-milk concoction made with cobra venom, I trusted him with my life. I drank it. Then I died.

My master had told me that our ultimate fear is death, and if I could experience death, I would conquer that fear forever.

"How is that possible?" I struggled to understand. "If you die, you don't come back to tell about it."

"There's a way," he said. "Meditation can kill the senses, and if you go into a deep enough trance, you can know what it is to die. If you do this, never again will you feel sadness for those who die. Never again will you fear death."

Our master chose five of us who were devoted to him. We were brought some Indian tea with milk and other ingredients. We didn't know what it was, except that one ingredient was poison from the fangs of a cobra.

I drink from the cup, gulping down every drop. About 30 seconds later, I feel my lungs close up and my heart shut down. Intense pain racks my body. I can't breathe, and I'm gripped by terrible fear.

"This is it. I'm really dying. Why did I do this?" As the pain intensifies, I think about all the people I love. I squirm and rock uncontrollably, as if in seizure. I fight it. Finally, I know I can fight no more. *"I'm done. I'm dead."* As soon as I let go, I see a white dot which grows to become a giant light that completely surrounds me and lifts me into the air. Am I imagining other people's descriptions of near-death experiences, or is this real? All I know is that I can't feel the ground beneath me or the air around me. I'm just floating in this beautiful realm of perfection. It's unlike anything I've ever experienced.

Then another cliché comes true. I actually see scenes from my life playing in front of me. I see my brothers and sisters and I see my schools, family meals. *"Wow, "this is beautiful. This is heaven. Why would I fight this? I never want to go back."*

The doctor who was monitoring me said I was clinically dead for many minutes. But during those minutes, I lived a million lifetimes. It was my first taste of what life is like for those who reach the seventh step.

Beyond the gateway to death, logic becomes irrelevant. You don't need to drink cobra venom to achieve this experience. Transcending each of the previous six steps will take you to the threshold, and you can cross over with a mind that is capable of focusing and then completely letting go.

You float. There's no sensation of anything touching you anywhere, not even clothing against your skin. You don't even remember if you are wearing clothes, but it doesn't matter. You might picture it as drifting in a warm spa, every muscle in your body completely relaxed; no, not relaxed, but gone. Your muscles, your body – they no longer seem to exist.

This is no ordinary meditation. The "warm spa" sensation isn't really warm, and no bubbles caress your skin. It's as if you were floating in water exactly matched to your body temperature. Your senses detect nothing different between outside and inside, so they send no message at all to your brain. No motion, no waves, no bubbles, no chill, no warmth. Complete neutrality. Nothing to report. All is calm.

Your body gradually melts away. You begin to experience what words cannot adequately convey – other than to call it death of the physical body. This isn't death in the earthly sense of pain or loss. It's more like your soul or consciousness has taken a complete and blissful departure. The corporeal concerns of the body cease to have relevance. You have entered Oneness, the highest realm of existence.

Your brain receives no stimuli from the ears, eyes, nose, mouth or skin. Bodily sensations hold no meaning for the place where your consciousness has gone. You are in a location without location. You see nothing, and yet you see everything. You are a being without being. You exist in a time without time.

You realize that you are not something, but everything. Your essence is the same infinitesimal energy that makes up all matter everywhere. Nothing separates you from anything else in the entire universe. You are truly one with the Absolute. You have transcended all the turning points in your life: Wanting, Giving, Receiving, Balance, Satisfaction and Detachment are all phases of your distant past. The feeling is pure peace. This is the end of your journey. No more searching, no more yearning, no more struggle. Your life will never be the same. You have acquired all the wisdom and inner peace you'll ever need.

It's as if you have been spending your whole life trying to put together a gigantic puzzle, yet you never could seem to get all the pieces to fit. Suddenly, the pieces fall neatly and effortlessly into place, and the picture becomes complete serenity.

Perhaps the most remarkable part of this experience is the

realization that you haven't really "achieved" anything. You merely returned to your source. Once you get there, you understand how easy it is.

I've seen the bright flash of the Big Bang and traveled forward through everything that has ever happened up to the present moment. These experiences are part of my core – and yours – because all of it happened to us. Or rather, it happened to the particles of which we are made. We are star stuff, composed of atoms forged in the furnaces of suns that burst into supernovae. The energy from which we arose contains a history, and that history is written inside every one of us. I personally experienced the replay of a cosmological journey that took almost 14 billion years.

After regaining full consciousness following my death by cobra venom, I slept for a day and a half and awoke with a smile ear to ear. For several days, I walked around in a trance, totally connected to nature. Birds would actually fly down and sit in my hand. The others who also drank the cobra venom tea had similar experiences.

Eventually, I glided back down into the material world, but I came away with a precious gift: a road map to wisdom and inner peace. I realized that death is a good and necessary part of nature, and ever since that day, I have felt no fear of dying, nor do I feel sadness for the deceased.

Deng Ming-Dao, author of "Gateway to a Vast World," wrote about our misconceptions of death in "365 Tao Daily Meditations." He says, "Nothing is ever destroyed. Nothing is ever created. All is infinity." The following is from his meditation on composure:

"For most people, killing is an abhorrence. If they had to kill, they would be horrified, and their emotions would be uncontrollable. Likewise, if they were being threatened with death, they would be afraid and would struggle to keep alive.

"Both these situations involve extreme attachment to what

we know and how we wish to remain. Both situations indicate a fundamentally limited view of the world. We assume that we are truly destroying something. But though this body may be slain, the soul cannot be slain. Every soul is but a part of the infinite, cosmic soul.

"You could subtract numerous souls from the world, and the number of souls would not be diminished. Numerous souls could be born, and the number of souls would not be augmented. Nothing is truly destroyed, and nothing is truly born. Only appearances change.

"Therefore, people of composure view the transformations of the world calmly. They do not become alarmed with the different permutations of phenomena. They know that these are all merely outer manifestations of an indefinable, unlimited and infinite reality."

The Pune experience left me with one overwhelming revelation: The dominant natural law of the universe is balance. All things are driven toward balance. Most of us live on a superficial level, so all we see are details. Cars, jobs, friends, TV, computers, weather, noise, pain, pleasure – our entire universe is just loud, banging details.

The 7 Steps to Wisdom and Inner Peace represent a turning point. They enable you to see beyond the details and experience the peace of balance. This kind of enlightenment can come in a split second, hitting you like a thunderbolt, but the Western mind usually has a tough time accepting this. Fighting it will only block you further.

I realize how crazy I must sound to skeptics who can't accept what I've described, but transcendental and mystical experiences like these have been part of our recorded history for thousands of years. I wasn't the first, and I won't be the last. There are many paths. This is mine. I offer it as a guide to help you take yours.

We've started this book with a description of The End. It's real, and it awaits you.

Chapter Two

YOU ARE EVERYTHING

Quantum physics thus reveals a basic oneness of the universe.
Fritjof Capra

What was the universe like before time began? Prior to the presumed Big Bang that led to all matter in the known universe, what was the nature of existence? It's the great mystery of our time. But our best evidence, theories and guesses all point toward a central idea: everything was once a single One. I believe this Oneness still remains as an interconnected whole, despite the fact that particles of the Oneness are farther apart than they once were.

Many physicists agree with this and have expressed it in theory and mathematical formulae. They call it "quantum entanglement," and in simple terms, it means they have measurable evidence that suggests everything in the universe is connected by an invisible "fabric" or unified field.

Scientists can trace the evolution of the expanding universe all the way back 13.7 billion years to that tiny point they call the singularity. Albert Einstein theorized that before the universe began, it was a gravitational singularity with infinite density. This is impossible for the human mind to imagine.

The best we can do is picture a single dot suspended in the void, and packed into this tiny dot was all the matter that comprises the entire universe as we know it today. All of this unimaginably immense universe, packed into a tiny point smaller than the dot beneath this question mark? It's a false picture, because we think in terms of physical laws, and at the point of a singularity – whether it's the origin of the universe or at the center of a black hole – physical laws break down. Even the science of quantum physics loses meaning at the point of the singularity.

Time, space and size are all relative terms. That is, they only exist in relation to something else. For example, time can't exist without change. If nothing changes, time can't be measured. If the singularity that once held all matter in the universe remained in a steady state without changing, there would be no difference between two seconds and two billion years. And if nothing else existed, the size of the singularity couldn't be measured. Was it the size of an atom or the combined size of 100 billion suns? Without an outside observer and nothing to which that observer can make a comparison, the entire concept of size is meaningless.

How was this singularity suspended in the void? Was there black space in three dimensions as we know it today? Most astrophysicists believe that space, time and matter all came into existence as the same moment – the moment we know as the Big Bang.

Some serious scientists believe that reality exists in at least 11 different dimensions, that parallel universes surround us, and that new universes are being created and extinguished all the time. Big Bangs may be commonplace.

The singularity before a Big Bang might be imagined as a perfect balance between positive and negative. It's like matter and anti-matter. They cancel each other out and create equilibrium. Nothing changes, and it's a perfect heaven. The singularity remains in this perfect state for an infinite amount of time, which is the same duration as no time at all, because without a measurement for time, there's no difference.

If, given this so-called infinite amount of time, all possibilities that can occur *will* occur, perhaps it was inevitable that matter and anti-matter would separate, triggering the Big Bang. Or you could choose to believe God touched off the Big Bang. In any case, this unleashed enormous energy with positive and negative charges. Immediately, as this energy coalesced into hydrogen and helium, the matter of the universe began seeking to re-balance itself. This universal imperative led to the structure we see throughout the cosmos today.

Since humans are just tiny expressions of this interconnected energy, we, too, are driven toward greater balance. It may not be readily apparent by the state of world affairs today, but achieving balance takes time. When the universe itself finally achieves balance, its matter and anti-matter may be rejoined as another singularity. When we as a species finally achieve balance, perhaps we'll all exist in Step 7 (Oneness) and live with wisdom and inner peace in a kind of heaven on Earth.

Fritjof Capra, author of "The Tao of Physics," said that "physicists do not need mysticism, and mystics do not need physics, but humanity needs both." That's exactly the approach needed in order to achieve a profound understanding of our 7 Steps to Wisdom and Inner Peace. Physicists and mystics both believe that they are finding truth, but neither thinks the other has the right access code. I believe they both do.

Science, religion and philosophy have all opened our eyes to truth, and it's remarkable how often they draw the same conclusions. (Physics is not my area of expertise, and my observations in all these areas are based on independent reading and research – with the exception of mystical experience, with which I have first-hand knowledge. I encourage the curious reader to explore sources in our "Works Cited" section and others.)

Although Capra's book drew criticism from physicist Jeremy Bernstein, Capra's parallels between mysticism and physics apparently made a positive impact on Werner Heisenberg, one of the founders of quantum physics.

"I had several discussions with Heisenberg," Capra told fellow author Renee Weber. "I showed him the whole manuscript chapter by chapter. He was very interested and very open, and he told me something that I think is not known publicly because he never published it. He said that he was well aware of these parallels. While he was working on quantum theory, he went to India to lecture and was a guest of Tagore (the Nobel Prize-winning Hindu poet and spiritual leader). He talked a lot with Tagore about Indian philosophy. Heisenberg told me that these talks had helped him a lot with his work in physics, because they showed him that all these new ideas in quantum physics were in fact not all that crazy.

He realized there was, in fact, a whole culture that subscribed to very similar ideas. Heisenberg said that this was a great help for him. Niels Bohr (Danish physicist and Nobel Prize winner) had a similar experience when he went to China."

Quantum physics is nothing more than a new attempt to come to grips with the universe. Max Planck, the Nobel Prize-winning father of quantum theory, came to the same conclusion as the transcendental mystics. "All matter originates and exists only by virtue of a force," Planck said. "We must assume behind this force the existence of a conscious and intelligent Mind. This Mind is the matrix of all matter."

Theologians would interpret that capital-M "Mind" as God, while the mystics see it as the Absolute Bliss Consciousness with which they seek unification.

In Buddhism and some other Eastern religions, you can become God yourself. They actually offer classes to guide you and teach you how. When I explored these classes, I noticed we students gradually all began to think alike. It raised the question in my mind: Why are the exact same thoughts coming to my mind as to these other minds?

At some point along our path, I remembered something my master had told me about this process: I am not inputting any new data into my brain or body. I'm reaching within myself and exploring what's inside. There's something deep within me, and within you and everybody else, that gives truth.

"Creation is like a puzzle," my master said. "It's a picture inside everybody. It comes in pieces, thousands of pieces scattered all over the place, and you look at those pieces in the environment, and that provides a reflection of yourself. You find the right pieces and put them together, and if you go over it, eventually you will have a perfect picture. And it doesn't matter who you are, you will have the exact same picture."

God is one name for that picture puzzle within us, and different so-called prophets at different times and places have told us various ways to get there and how to put that puzzle together. The picture was always there, and whenever the prophets encountered mystical experiences they couldn't explain in ways that others would understand, they said, "Just believe. If you believe it, you're going to get there."

That puzzle picture is encoded in our DNA: It's a map of the universe. It's a map of the path toward creating perfect balance. Every being and every elementary particle in the universe contains this same map, this same drive to create balance. This balance can be described as perfection.

In Western cultures, we're taught that your natural, inborn goal should be to "get as much as you can." Heaven is the most money, the biggest house, the fastest car. But hard-wired into your genes, in a cosmic fingerprint left by the Big Bang of Creation, a different message cries to be heard. That message is the primal urge for balance and unity in all things. That's where true wisdom and inner peace lie. That's heaven.

Once you establish a sense of direction and purpose, you can move through the 7 Steps with joy and ease. You realize we all belong to each other. This is our social divination, our force of nature that will guide everyone and everything into the path toward Oneness.

It's impossible to be in the 7th Step and still desire wealth and material success and "getting as much as you can." You're balanced, satisfied, detached and at one with all that we call existence. You live with divine understanding of Creation and the interconnectedness of all things.

Will we as a civilization all be able to share in this sublime wisdom and inner peace before we destroy ourselves with war, pollution, disease and starvation? It's an open question, but the Earth is destined for destruction nonetheless. The sun won't burn forever, and our world will become uninhabitable by these fragile, watery skin bags we call our bodies.

What lies beyond our inevitable destruction is the vast universe to which we belong. We have always been a part of this universe, and we always will be. Matter can neither be created nor destroyed. The Cosmic Consciousness persists.

Someday, time may stop again as our universe collapses into a Big Crunch. Perhaps our single Cosmic Consciousness includes all possible universes in all possible dimensions, and we may be part of that whole organism. When our questions tug at the edge of infinity, they escape the grasp of a puny human neocortex. But deeper inside, beyond the logic of the primate brain, the secrets of the Absolute live within your elementary particles of energy.

The universe lives within you, and you live within the universe. There is no difference. Our destiny is to complete the circle, to become one with that Cosmic Consciousness, as we once were. If you can fulfill your destiny now and become balanced before your body dies and turns to dust, you can exist in a living heaven. We call it heaven because that word has a certain meaning in your mind, but the people we've seen at the level of Oneness are not really people anymore. They laugh, they look like people, but they're different beings. They are the universe.

You can do the same. You can become everything. And once you do, our civilization will have taken one more step toward wisdom and inner peace.

Chapter Three

NO SECRET

"We are all connected, and we are all One."
Rhonda Byrne

"The Secret" by Rhonda Byrne enlightened millions to concepts that date back 3,000 years. They were really no secret, as the author herself points out with references to sources like Charles Haanel's "Master Key System" from 1912, Prentice Mulford's 19th-century "Thoughts Are Things" and Robert Collier's "Secret of the Ages" from 1926. The first ideological spark for Byrne's movie and DVD was said to be a 1910 book by Wallace D. Wattles called "The Science of Getting Rich."

This is not a sequel to "The Secret," nor is it a parody or harsh criticism of the book or film. But we believe "The Secret" falls a bit short because it deals predominantly with just the first two of our 7 Steps to Wisdom and Inner Peace – Wanting and Having. It focuses heavily on wealth enhancement. If you stop there, you'll never experience the bliss that awaits you in the spiritual levels of Balance, Satisfaction, Detachment and Oneness.

Wanting and Having, in the long run, are actually harmful to your pursuit of wisdom and inner peace. Many enlightened people have reported feeling skeptical of or even repelled by Byrnes' emphasis on material wealth. Come along on this journey, and we'll show you a place so fantastic that it renders all the material wealth in the world petty and insignificant.

We fully understand the emphasis on money. "Time Magazine" quoted one of the backers of "The Secret" film as saying, "We desired to hit the masses, and money is the number one thing on the masses' minds."

The decision to call Byrne's material "The Secret" and use imagery reminiscent of "The Da Vinci Code" – one of the best-selling novels of all time – proved brilliant. Her marketing team capitalized on the public's hunger for ancient mystery, then dressed it up with fake parchment, quill-and-ink fonts resembling Leonardo Da Vinci's own hand, and faux sealing wax. Publishers aren't shy about cashing in on the success of previous best-sellers.

"It was an incredibly savvy move to call it 'The Secret'," said Donavin Bennes, a buyer who specializes in metaphysics for Borders Books. "We all want to be in on a secret."

This book falls into the same genre as Rhonda Byrnes' work – metaphysical self-help – and presumably will attract a like-minded audience. The point is to get the message into the hands – and minds – of as many people as possible, so we applaud the groundwork laid by "The Secret." The concepts in Rhonda Byrnes' book can work for you, and the impact of her book on the human condition has been mostly positive.

While the 7 Steps to Wisdom and Inner Peace are original and expressed here for the first time, their well-water springs from belief systems that are also thousands of years old. We distilled their essence from the science, philosophy and spiritual beliefs of many civilizations, and today we stand on the shoulders of giants to present these ideas to you.

That's no secret.

Chapter Four

WISDOM AND INNER PEACE?

*The intuitive mind is a sacred gift, and the rational mind is a
faithful servant.
We have created a society that honors the servant and has forgotten
the gift.*
Albert Einstein

What do we mean by inner peace? How do we define wisdom? We
must answer these two important questions before we unfurl the
road map showing you how to get there.

We endeavored to give you a glimpse of inner peace in our
opening chapter. The sense of fulfillment and joy is overwhelming
and, at the same time, completely natural. It feels normal. It feels
right. It feels like you've come home.

In sports, enlightened coaches and athletes talk of being "in the
zone." They perform almost without any conscious thought.
Everything just falls into place effortlessly. Musicians experience
the same sensation when they just "feel" their music and let go.
Flawless performances emerge when you're "in the flow."

After all the coaching, training and studying have served their
purpose, at some point the student must allow the information to
seep into the subconscious. You clear your head and actually
become the experience.

A baseball coach tells his batters to "see the ball, *be* the ball."
When the batter can stop thinking about every little detail and
become one with his surroundings, connecting with a fast-moving,
spinning, 6-inch ball suddenly seems easier. It's all part of you.
Even athletes who know nothing about meditation can accept and
use this technique to excel in golf, tennis, soccer, or any other
endeavor.

When you reach the apex, you don't *have* inner peace, you *are*
inner peace. Right now, only two things stand between you and

this wonderful place: Fear and desire. Those two primal drives keep humans perpetually on-edge. All our other inner urges can be traced back to one of those two big motivators, which we developed long ago as survival instincts.

We seek food and shelter because we fear starvation and vulnerability. Desire drives us to bond with the opposite sex, which ensures the survival of the species. We attack other tribes because we fear they might attack us first. We desire more of everything, which will make us powerful enough to conquer all our fears.

Fear and desire push us as individuals and as neighborhoods, tribes, teams, corporations and states. All the nation-building and civilization advancement throughout history can be laid at the feet of fear or desire. Those motivate us to constantly keep moving. So why would anybody want to lose these motivators? Haven't they been responsible for all that's good in the world?

That's certainly one way to look at it, but there's another. To be sure, desire (another word for Wanting, which is Step 1 on our journey) led us to develop philosophy, science, religion, art, music and literature. They sprang from our desire for clarity, knowledge, meaning, beauty, rhythm and expression.

Fear, meanwhile, motivated us to develop medicine, laws, government and advanced construction ... even the Space Race that culminated with man walking on the moon was motivated by fear over whether the Soviets or Americans would rule the skies, the ultimate high ground.

But here's the other way to look at it: for all the advancement they spurred, fear and desire are also to blame for all the wars and bloodshed that have ever occurred since before Homo Sapiens could even form words. Fear and desire ignite mistrust of our fellow man and rightly so. If those around you fear you or desire what you have, you'd be a fool to trust them ... unless you can break free from the shackles of fear and desire. Only then, when you no longer fear death, nor desire more than you already have, can you be absolutely free. You become immune to the primitive drives of all those around you. You "don't get caught up in that game."

In order to evolve as a species, we'll have to move beyond fear and desire. Only then will we qualify to be considered "civilized."

This brings us to the second question of this chapter: How do we define wisdom? Wisdom is the innate apprehension of inner peace. It's not necessarily acquired by book-learning or doctoral degrees. It's just a special illumination that gives you deep, profound insight. This illumination could derive from education, travel, experience (hence, the proverbial "wise old man") or any number of pursuits, but when wisdom finally begins to blossom, inner peace is the result.

We use "innate apprehension" to describe that concept of the athlete or musician who absorbs all coaching, training and study, then lets it all go and *becomes* the experience. When that happens to you, wisdom manifests itself as deep "knowing" that transcends words. You feel it and know it's real, but you probably won't be able to talk about it coherently. That's part of the challenge in writing this book. How do we put into words these exhilarating experiences, this innate apprehension? How do we communicate what we feel on such a deep, unspoken level?

Lao Tzu wrote: "The Tao that can be told is not the eternal Tao. The name that can be named is not the eternal name. The nameless is the beginning of heaven and earth. The named is the mother of ten thousand things. Ever desireless, one can see the mystery. Ever desiring, one can see the manifestations."

The fascinating parallel to that cryptic message is that it was originally written in Chinese pictographs, which are impossible to translate cleanly into English. So when you read translations of the entire "Tao Te Ching," you'll see wildly different versions. Chinese pictographs express concepts that can be absorbed and felt with enough contemplation, which can lead to wisdom, but one can't simply write a few English sentences and expect to communicate innate apprehension.

For example, here's another, breezier translation of that same opening to the "Tao Te Ching," this one by Ron Hogan: "If you can talk about it, it ain't Tao. If it has a name, it's just another thing.

Tao doesn't have a name. Names are for ordinary things. Stop wanting stuff. It keeps you from seeing what's real. When you want stuff, all you see are things. These two statements have the same meaning. Figure them out, and you've got it made."

Ah, it makes a little more sense now, perhaps ... but whose version is more accurate? We compare it to words in other languages that have no English translation whatsoever, like *simpatico* in Spanish. A person who is *simpatico* is pleasant, nice, agreeable, likeable, congenial ... but something more than that, too. You have to experience the language and the people for a while before the full meaning of *simpatico* sinks in. It's like trying to describe what a *mensch* is to someone who doesn't speak Yiddish. The best way to describe a *mensch* to someone who speaks Spanish is to say he's *simpatico* ... and yet, that doesn't tell the whole story, either.

We have a profoundly exciting journey ahead of us. When the wisdom and inner peace rise within you, the feeling may leave you overwhelmed and speechless. But before we can *be* the experience, we need a little background on the roots of wisdom ... in words that bear some clarity.

Chapter Five

PHILOSOPHY

Everything is but a dream within a dream.
Edgar Allen Poe

Where have all the philosophers gone? Apparently, they have gone to graveyards, every one. A subjective list of the 20 most prominent philosophers of all time can be found in "An Incomplete Education" by Judy Jones and William Wilson. Sixteen of those philosophers died before 1900, and all the rest died before 1953. It seems that not a single superstar of pure thought has taken a breath since the mid-20th century. Maybe it's because philosophy doesn't pay very well.

Georg Hegel, one of our personal favorites, wrote "The Philosophy of Right" and managed to achieve wealth, fame and favors from the King of Prussia, but all of that happened around the turn of the 18th century. His books, filled with complex prose and the occasional invented word, couldn't crack a bestseller list today.

What is philosophy, and why doesn't anybody make a living at it anymore? Philosophy is the study of everything that counts. It is the search for what really matters. Ranked chronologically, the first two philosophers on Jones' and Wilson's list are Plato and Aristotle, ancient Greeks who laid the foundation for all who were to follow. British mathematician and logician Alfred North Whitehead said that "philosophy is only a series of footnotes to Plato." But then, much of what Plato wrote was a recounting of Socrates, who talked a lot but never wrote anything down. Nobody knows where "the study of everything that counts" really started.

But perhaps we can trace its end. Originally, philosophers examined the structure of matter, the existence of gods and the nature of good and evil. They spent lifetimes speculating on subjects that were stuck in the realm of metaphysics. These were questions without provable answers, so they were fair game for philosophy.

Eventually, astronomers disproved the existence of a physical "heaven above," and physicists answered most of our questions about the structure of matter. Theologians walked away with the rest of it: God, good and evil.

Philosophers shuffled off into the margins of society. In 1950s America, they donned black beatnik garb and debated the nature of existence in coffeehouses, fueled by caffeine and the writings of Allen Ginsburg and Jack Kerouac.

In the Sixties, beatniks morphed into hippies, and the focus moved East, with the Mahareshi Mahesh Yogi preaching his Science of Being and the Art of Living. When The Beatles became transfixed by the Mahareshi's message, popular philosophy was reduced to a simple but beautiful phrase: All you need is love. But then the Mahareshi allegedly groped for a little too much love from some of his young and pretty followers, and the flower-power fad started to wilt.

In the Seventies, thousands of seekers (including me) followed the Bhagwan Shree Rajneesh, who led a movement that began in India and migrated to the United States in 1981. Rajneesh opposed the established religions. He found his truth from various sources, including Buddha, Krishna, Jesus, Socrates, Zen masters and Jewish Hassids. Rajneesh said the greatest values in life are love, meditation and laughter, and that the goal of human life was to reach spiritual enlightenment.

But his message got swallowed by controversy. Rajneesh fled India to elude income tax evasion charges, and later he was arrested in North Carolina for immigration crimes. Members of his "Rajneeshees" organization also were charged with the attempted murder of the Bhagwan's personal physician. Rajneesh himself (then calling himself Osho) claimed he was poisoned in jail, leading to his slow death four years later, in 1990. His ashes now rest in Pune, India, where I first met him.

Where does all this leave the state of philosophy today?

Remarkably, it seems that today's philosophers are the quantum physicists. Examine their breathtaking theories of parallel universes, 11 dimensions of reality, and vibrating strings – infinitesimally small strands of energy that are believed to unify all matter in the universe.

These theories lend credence to our own philosophy, as expressed in Chapter 2 (You Are Everything) and Chapter 18 (The Living Universe). Joseph Lyken, a theoretical particle physicist at the Fermi National Accelerator Laboratory in Illinois, appreciates the fine line between science and philosophy. "How do you test string theory?" he asks. "If you can't test it in the way we test in normal theories, it's not science. It's philosophy."

Traditionally, philosophers have held sway over these five areas of intellectual examination:

Logic: what makes sense and what doesn't. What's valid and what's invalid, as determined by critical reasoning.

Ethics: Sometimes called the science of morality. Ethical behavior is "doing the right thing." Values are assigned as good or bad.

Aesthetics: Another value judgment like ethics. Here, you can debate whether beauty is objective or subjective, and examine whether there is a relationship between beauty and goodness.

Epistemology: Do we really know anything, and if so, how do we know that we know it? Are you really reading this book, or are you dreaming that you are reading it?

Metaphysics: This is the realm in which we will weave the primary message of this book. It's the study of being and knowing. Literally, it comes from the Greek "meta" (beyond) and "physics" (nature). Another definition of metaphysics: "A field of abstract thought and philosophy about topics beyond the physical level of understanding. This includes subjects like existence, the soul, being, the supernatural and psychic phenomena."

While we will delve into many areas that invite you to think beyond the limits of your five senses, "Travel Within" is not like so many New Age books that give blind credence to theories about alchemy, astrology, the power of crystals, geomancy, teleportation or time travel. We will veer away from topics that blatantly defy logic or science, otherwise passing no judgment on such pursuits. But the message here definitely fits into the category of philosophy. It's a firm belief – or hypothesis, if you will – built on systematic observation. The conclusions we've reached transcend science and religion (topics covered in subsequent chapters), although they contain elements of both.

We could spend the rest of this chapter examining the historical progression of philosophy and the roots of wisdom which have led us to what (and how) we think today, but other books and other authors are much better suited to that endeavor. We encourage you to seek them out. You'll find several listed in the "Works Cited" section at the back of this book.

So instead, let's take a short journey of the mind into areas that may seem far away from science, which is the subject of our next chapter (That's where we will return to the world of verifiable facts and provable hypotheses, and we'll explore how they support the conclusions we've drawn). But right now, please humor me. Close your eyes and take three very deep breaths, exhaling slowly after each. Done? You should feel a little light-headed, a little tingly in your fingers. It's just extra oxygen in your bloodstream. That's physical science. But when your brain "breathes" deeply, it operates more efficiently – as long as you don't hyperventilate and fall over. And when your mind is open, it, too, functions at a higher level.

With a fully oxygenated brain and an open mind, let's consider the different philosophies of what we call the East and West, and see if we agree that they lead to the same place. More importantly, if we can agree that they both share the same destination, perhaps we will realize that with the fullness of this understanding, all becomes neutral. And with neutrality comes peace.

In India, almost everyone is a philosopher. The country is so poor and overpopulated that people spend much of their time with eyes focused inward, examining the deep questions. When you live close to the ground, at subsistence level, your priorities become much different from those in the West. Few in India worry about whether their lips are too thin or their hips are too fat.

The air in Kolkata (formerly Calcutta) lies heavy with dust, smoke and stench. Sacred cows defecate in the streets, and so do naked children. Kolkata's Hugli River runs black with oil and smelly debris. Oppressive heat and starving beggars weigh heavily on every unsuspecting Western newcomer. Yet here, as in other, more fortunate Indian cities, the people believe in following a path to Brahman – the Infinite Being or ultimate reality. They believe your karma (what you do) determines your fate.

In the West, the same belief is expressed in this fashion: "As you sow, so shall you reap." Westerners believe the path to righteousness is filled with good deeds, not just good thoughts. (We use "righteousness" in this book to mean "in accordance with virtue or morality," without any religious connotation whatsoever.)

The air in New York City weighs hot, dirty and damp on your skin during summer. The odors of urine and unwashed vagabonds rise from alleys and gutters. The East River roils with garbage and the occasional dead body, shocking the unsuspecting foreign visitor.

It is not Kolkata, but to the perceptive eye, similarities abound.

On April 8, 1966, the cover of Time Magazine asked, "Is God Dead?" For the rest of that century, America continued to drift in an increasingly secular direction, at least from a Middle Eastern perspective. But the West's basic philosophy never really changed. The goal has always been to "do the right thing," even in the minds of angry urbanites like Spike Lee. Putting aside extremists and terrorists, we find that most people all over the world share a sense of obligation, or at least a desire, to do good.

Their definitions of good look remarkably similar, too. The Noble Eightfold Path followed in much of Asia calls for cultivation in three areas: wisdom, ethical conduct and mental development. The eight goals are righteousness in view, intention, speech, action, livelihood, effort, mindfulness and concentration. In

Western tradition, we have seven virtues to counter the so-called seven deadly sins. Those virtues are humility, kindness, moderation, purity, patience, generosity and diligence. The exact words vary depending on whether you consult secular or Roman Catholic sources, but the intent remains the same.

When you strip away all Eastern mysticism and Western dogma, you find that most people everywhere share a desire to live in peace and conduct themselves in accordance with values that likely would be termed "good" in any language.

The differences that separate tribes and nations seem petty when our minds are elevated to the philosophical level. We're fighting over land, resources or religious ideology, and we're motivated mostly by fear.

None of these would be important issues in a global village where all people shared the same philosophical goals. And the crazy thing is we already do share the same philosophical goals! Travel to almost any nation on Earth, spend enough time there to get the culture under your fingernails, and that's the truth you'll find deep inside. Superficial differences can be bridged easily. On a strictly philosophical level, and we're all basically on the same page (excluding, of course, the lunatic fringe).

The late Leo Buscaglia, Ph.D., and former Professor of Education at the University of Southern California, wrote: "Discovery of self is a universal quest and a state of being that brings with it the power to experience the texture of life with greater intensity and sensitivity."

Isn't this a philosophy we all share? We want to know what makes us tick, and why. We ache for understanding, and we crave peace. At this moment, we're engaged in a race to achieve mutual understanding before we destroy ourselves. Does that sound alarmist or archaic? Some say the seeds of World War III were planted by al Qaeda on 9/11/01, and the escalation was marked by rising violence during the ensuing years in Afghanistan, Iraq, North Korea, Iran, Israel, Sudan ...

Since the collapse of the Soviet Union, CIA analysts say the primary threat to America is nuclear capability in the hands of a small radical faction. CIA senior intelligence analyst Michael Scheuer wrote that no one should be surprised when al Qaeda detonates a weapon of mass destruction in the United States. Is it inevitable? "I don't believe in inevitability," Scheuer said. "But I think it's pretty close to being inevitable. A nuclear weapon of some dimension, whether it's actually a nuclear weapon or a dirty bomb or some kind of radiological device? Yes, I think it's probably a near thing."

Imagine a peaceful counterpoint to that dangerous path – a growing understanding that the core philosophies of most Jews, Muslims, Christians, Hindus, Buddhists and atheists are strikingly similar in at least one vital way: We want to follow a path of right-eousness that leads to peace.

To reach this understanding, we must slash and burn the perceived differences between tribes. This starts on a grassroots level, but it's really nothing more than simple education. Our wish is that the message of this book and others like it can help. What we hate or fear, we usually don't understand. If a deep level of mutual understanding could spread, people would begin to experience a sense of neutrality. We're not suggesting they will all "love thy neighbor" (although wouldn't that be nice?), but with simple neutrality comes peace.

Imagine a large group of people – your group – walking toward a goal. It could be Mecca, Mission Beach or a McDonald's restaurant. But as you walk, 6.5 billion other people are walking, too. They're all in different groups, all heading toward the same destination. It's not a race. There's enough room at this destination for everybody. You all come from different locations, wear different clothes and speak different languages. But you all have the same goal.

You don't care who gets there first. You're completely neutral about these other people. And that brings you a sense of peace about them, because you know they won't try to stop you or harm you. You understand that they want the same thing you want, and it comes in unlimited supply: Peace, happiness, freedom. There's enough to go around for everybody. To be certain, this is a simple-minded philosophy. Nobody said it has to be complicated. But it does have firm roots in science.

Chapter Six

SCIENCE

The greatest discoveries of science have always been those that
forced us to rethink our beliefs about the universe and our place in it.
Robert L. Park

Scientists generally don't like to get involved in discussions of philosophy or religion. Their passion is devoted to subjects that can be tested and proven. As an electrical engineer, I share that passion. We need to know how electricity will behave under given conditions, and there's little room for speculation. We have to understand the imbalance of electrons and protons if we wish to harness this powerful force and light up your plasma big-screen television.

Science is a branch of knowledge based on objectivity, involving observation and experimentation. At its heart lies the scientific method, which you probably learned in grade school as this series of steps: (1) identify a problem you would like to solve, (2) formulate a hypothesis, (3) test the hypothesis, (4) collect and analyze the data, and (5) draw conclusions.

Theologians and philosophers sometimes mock science when it posits theories that turn out to be wrong, but in our view, the flexibility and open-mindedness of science is actually its greatest strength. Faced with a new set of facts, a scientist is much quicker to abandon a faulty theory than a theologian or philosopher, whose belief systems operate outside the realm of measurable data.

Civilization's bright minds once used their powers of observation to conclude that the Earth was flat, that the appearance of a comet meant disaster would soon follow, and that if raw meat were left to rot, it would spontaneously generate life in the form of maggots.

Experimentation proved all these theories wrong, and science happily moved forward. The "Travel Within" hypothesis we've formed as a recipe for inner peace is also based on scientific principles, and we are convinced that it will not end up alongside flat-Earth theory. (Incidentally, the Flat Earth Society may finally be wobbling; one of their Internet sites has gone defunct with the message that the Web page "seems to have fallen off the edge of the Earth, along with its maintainer.")

Writing in the year 63 C.E., Roman author Lucius Seneca observed, "There will come a time when our descendants will be amazed that we did not know things that are so plain to them ... Our universe is a sorry little affair unless it has in it something for every age to investigate ... Nature does not reveal her mysteries once and for all."

Thanks to the rigorous observation and testing of science – as well as its open-minded flexibility – Seneca's prediction has been borne out innumerable times. We know that the Earth revolves around the Sun, not vice versa; that thunder is caused by the collisions of molecules, not angry gods; and that when a person has a headache, drilling holes in the skull to let out the demons isn't always the best medicine.

But Seneca was wise to suggest that our universe has something "for every age to investigate," because we still can't prove the Big Bang theory about how the universe began, nor can we reliably predict how – or if – it will end. It may turn out that the "Travel Within" hypothesis can never be scientifically proved. Admittedly, our recipe for inner peace may shift from science to philosophy at the stage of experimentation, and in that respect, it's not unlike string theory. How can we measure and quantify an individual's psychological transformation?

But we can measure results. If our civilization uses this approach to achieve balance and harmony, as measured in decreasing numbers of wars and attacks on personal freedom, that will be scientific enough for me.

Philosopher David Hume insisted that nothing can be proved, and he may have been right, but rather than get bogged down in such sophistry, we can use the legal yardstick: "proved beyond a reasonable doubt." And if a worldwide peace movement springs from the "philosophy" in these pages, we would welcome its judgment by a jury of our peers.

Cosmologists will tell you they now accept Big Bang theory as being established, if not proved, beyond reasonable doubt. The discovery of Cosmic Background Radiation, which had been predicted by George Gamow in 1948 as a remnant of the Big Bang, seemed to silence critics who argued for Steady State Theory.

Remember that blockbuster question on the cover of Time magazine in 1966: Is God Dead? The subject was examined by no less a scientist than Stephen Hawking, widely regarded as the world's most brilliant theoretical physicist since Albert Einstein. Hawking's conclusion? If our current theories about the universe (many of which now seem "proved beyond a reasonable doubt") are correct, then Hawking wanted to know: "What place, then, for a creator?"

In his view, science can explain almost everything. Hawking wouldn't claim God doesn't exist – only that there seems to be nothing for Him to do. It's a thought that might shake theologians to the bone. But an alternative exists. What if Stephen Hawking, you, me, that rock, those trees and everything else in the universe were all God? Or, since we promised that the "Travel Within" approach would be essentially religion-free, you could call it "The Force" or "The Way."

The idea that God is the universe has a deep following in Hinduism. It's often called pantheism. While some forms of pantheism had their beginnings in religion, others have been based on scientific, philosophic or poetic points of view.

Pre-Socratic Greek philosopher Xenophanes (c.570–c.480 B.C.E.) speculated that God is the universe, and Stoicism, a school of philosophy founded by Zeno of Citium (c.300 B.C.E.), expanded on that theme. Pantheism can be found in the idealistic philosophy of German writers Hegel, Fichte, von Schelling and Schleiermacher. Although philosophical Taoism also carries pantheistic overtones, the view has been called atheistic, as well.

Philosopher-poet Samuel Taylor Coleridge argued that "every thing God, and no God, are identical positions."

So it doesn't have to be religious. But can it be scientific? Yes, if you call this all-inclusive entity "The Force," then the work of British physicist David Bohm will support that conclusion. Bohm, a protégé of Einstein's, developed an alternative explanation for why particles act the way they do on the quantum level. He called it "the quantum potential force," and Bohm believed it connects all things in the universe simultaneously.

He described it very much like "The Force" in George Lucas' "Star Wars" movies, with which Bohm (who died in 1992) was familiar. Bohm didn't suggest that Jedi masters like Yoda would be capable of controlling this force with their minds, but he was thoroughly convinced it exists.

Unlike other forces, the quantum potential force doesn't weaken as the distance between quantum-connected particles increases. According to Bohm's calculations, this force connects specific particles and can be disrupted but not shielded. The quantum potential force depends on a pattern of information that is beyond space and time. In simple terms, he was saying that everything is connected to everything else in a real, measurable way – which forms the very basis of our "Travel Within" hypothesis. If this sounds goofy or offends your sense of logic, you're starting to join the club of quantum physics. UC Berkeley professor Timothy Ferris, who wrote the PBS program "The Creation of the Universe," said that "the longer you look at quantum physics, the stranger it gets." And Nobel Prize-winning physicist Niels Bohr (1885-1962) felt that "if someone says that he can think about quantum physics without becoming dizzy, that shows only that he has not understood anything whatever about it."

Bohm's theory remains controversial, but it predicts the same results as standard quantum mechanics, and those results have been proven experimentally. So we have different paths in physics that end up at the same destination. That's the same model we posited for our civilization's journey to wisdom and inner peace: It doesn't matter whether you get there via philosophy or science, as long as you get there. Many choose the path of religion.

Chapter Seven

RELIGION

It's like a finger pointing at the moon.
If you stare at the finger, you miss all the heavenly glory.
Bruce Lee

We've made the assertion that all spiritual paths lead to the same destination. This is by no means a universally accepted assumption. Just try gathering confirmed Muslims, Catholics, Jews, Buddhists and Hindus into a small room and ask them to convince all the others that theirs is the one true faith.

Then get out of the way. Assuming they aren't armed and dangerous, the debate likely will last until they all run out of food, drink or breath, but it won't be resolved. That's because one can't follow any of those paths along fundamental lines and simultaneously accept that another path might be true. The conviction that they alone have the right answer is endemic to each of those mindsets.

But the beauty of the "Travel Within" hypothesis is that it doesn't matter whether you believe in a particular religion or not – you can still accept and follow our seven-step course to wisdom and inner peace. It should make sense to you whether you believe in no god, many gods, or one God.

"There is only one religion, though there are a hundred versions of it," said George Bernard Shaw, winner of the Nobel Prize for Literature in 1925. We appreciate the fact that all those fundamentalists locked in debate over which is the one true faith will never accept Shaw's proclamation, and in some sense that's not even relevant to our goal. But it's important to examine religion because our seven-step path is definitely a spiritual belief system that leads to a "promised land" of sorts, and once you reach Step 7 your viewpoint will be different. You'll be standing atop a metaphorical mountain.

We mentioned earlier that some of the precepts in this journey will be challenging and controversial. Here's one example: if a Wahhabi Muslim were to reach Step 7, he could no longer believe that Sunnis, Shi'ites, Jews, Christians and all other non-Wahhabis are nothing more than infidels who deserve to die for their sins. Instead, he would be neutral to all others and at peace with himself and the universe around him.

His picture of reality will have changed. But then, Wahhabis are said to be responsible for a majority of the Islamic terrorist acts of our time, so we don't apologize for shaking their religious tree. Most of the rest of us live in a vast Middle Earth where peaceful co-existence is possible without abandoning personal religious beliefs. So let's examine some of the major faiths. What do they have in common, where do they part company, and what role to they play in our seven-step process?

In the beginning, our gods were the Sun, Moon, Stars and Trees. At least, that's what archaeology tells us, and if we are to have a fair and balanced discussion of religion, we can't ignore the evidence.

Nobody can pinpoint the exact beginning of religion. Mankind traces its own written record back about 7,500 years, but our species has been around at least twenty times longer than that, and more than half a million years ago, prehistoric man was burying his dead with worldly goods which seem to have been preparations for an afterlife. Archaeologist Frederick Everard Zeuner said that 500,000-year-old burial caves in China contained artifacts of religious practices clustered around the deceased. Stone totems that were carved 30,000 years ago appear to pay homage to well-endowed Earth Mothers or fertility gods.

About 5,000 years ago, tribes of the Old Kingdom Dynasty in Egypt practiced primitive local religions featuring over 50 different gods. Whenever one tribe became politically dominant, its particular god also became dominant. Most of these deities were represented by animals, but as Egyptian civilization advanced, the gods took on human characteristics. Many gods were depicted with animal heads atop human bodies.

About that same time, Aryans settled on the banks of the Indus River and are now credited with having introduced a new belief system to the locals. It featured many gods, but seemed more like a way of life or spiritual discipline, as opposed to the nature-based homage of earlier religions. Hinduism was born. The word "Hindu" derives from the river Indus, which flows through northern India. In ancient times, the river was called the Sindhu, but Persians who migrated to India couldn't pronounce that, so they called the river Hindu, the land Hindustan, and its people Hindus.

Hinduism is the oldest major religion still in practice today, but it's actually something more than a religion in the Western sense. Perhaps it can best be defined as a way of life based on the teachings of ancient sages and scriptures like the Vedas and the Upanishads. Its core belief is that the ultimate reality (Brahman) is an impersonal Oneness.

After spending much time in India, I came away with an appreciation of Hinduism, so perhaps it's not surprising that elements of its philosophy will be recognizable in our 7 Steps to Wisdom and Inner Peace, but just as Rajneesh did before me, I have moved away from traditional, religious Hinduism.

Like almost all major religions, Hinduism has evolved and splintered into dozens of sects, each with its own different subset of beliefs. Many of these sects worship different gods, from Vishnu to Devi to Ganesh to the Sun-God.

Perhaps the sect of Hinduism most familiar to westerners is the Hare Krishna, also called the Chaitanyas. They sometimes hang around airports with their robes, beads and shaved heads, begging for money. Their chants were popularized in rock songs by George Harrison and The Culture Club, among others.

If you watched the TV comedy series "Dharma and Greg," you're familiar with another Hindu term. Dharma can be roughly translated as "that which supports the universe," which means any path of spiritual discipline that leads to God. Although dharma is often considered a Buddhist term, it found its beginnings in Hinduism. That would seem a natural transition into a quick look at Buddhism, but instead, we'll move chronologically to the second major religion to survive into contemporary times – Judaism.

All that stuff we said about the human species dating back half a million years? Forget it. According to Jewish tradition, Earth and the heavens didn't even exist until roughly 5,800 years ago. Creation occurred in 3760 B.C.E., and about 1,800 years later, a Sumerian named Abraham began to tell everyone that there is only one Almighty God (whose unspeakable name was later revealed as Yahweh).

Judaism's Holy Scripture is the Torah, the same work known to Christians as the Old Testament. While Jews have been persecuted, exiled and demonized over the millennia, there's no question that most modern western religions today, including Christianity, evolved from Judaism. Using the word "evolved" in the same sentence as Judaism is intentional, because it gives us an opportunity to segue into an important issue: Orthodox Jews don't believe in human evolution. They accept the account in Genesis as literal truth, including the Creation, Adam and Eve.

But, like Hinduism, various sects of Judaism began breaking off almost from the beginning. Today, Reform Jews and even many Conservative Jews interpret the Old Testament in more symbolic ways, leaving ample room for the acceptance of evolution.

Judah, the southern land in ancient Israel from which Judaism derives its name, became a major center for Yahwism (the early form of Judaism), which broke away from other sects like the Samaritans and the Rechabites. By 400 B.C.E., various forms of Judaism had been established in Babylonia (modern Iraq) and Egypt, and within 500 years, the religion had spawned other branches represented by the Sadducees, Essenes, Pharisees and Zealots.

Of these, the Pharisees were the most influential, and it was from them that both Christianity and Talmudic Judaism finally emerged. The first Christians were Palestinian Jews who became smitten (figuratively) by a rabbi named Jesus who spoke of universal love, the brotherhood of man and redemption through faith.

While Jews have every right to *kvetch* about persecution, the Christians endured plenty of problems of their own, not the least of which was being fed to lions for sport by the Romans. The Christian era got off to an inauspicious start when Emperor Claudius expelled all Christians from Rome, branding their theology as a dangerous and rebellious cult. Many stayed, at their own peril.

Under Nero, Christians were arrested and sentenced to be torn apart by animals, burned as human torches to light the evening skies, or crucified. The crucifixion of Jesus himself is seen by most Christians as an act of self-sacrifice to atone for mankind's sins and to restore believers to the love and friendship of God. Christ's resurrection from the dead is said to have reconciled humanity with God, granting eternal life in Heaven to the faithful. This information was handed down through a collection of writings that came to be known as the New Testament, which combines with the Old Testament of Judaism to form the Christian Bible.

Meanwhile, completely different flavors of religion were spreading throughout Asia – Zoroastrianism, Buddhism, Confucianism and Taoism. Hinduism influenced these movements, and all had distinct similarities: each was deeply philosophical in nature, and each sprang from the works of a human being.

The oldest is Zoroastrianism, founded in my native Persia around 1000 B.C.E. by Zarathustra. You may have heard the name if you're familiar with the soundtrack to Arthur C. Clarke's "2001: A Space Odyssey." The title theme is a classical piece by Strauss called "Also Spracht Zarathustra," sometimes erroneously translated as "Thus Spoke God." Zarathustra was considered a prophet, but his god was Ahura Mazda.

Zarathustra focused on the dualism of good and evil as both a cosmic one between Ahura Mazda and the evil spirit of violence and death, Angra Mainyu, and as an ethical dualism within the human consciousness. Zarathustra's teachings were subtle and sophisticated, but Persian Zoroastrianism was virtually wiped out by Moslem hordes in the eighth century. Survivors escaped to India and now call themselves Parsis.

Dualism also played prominently in the rise of Buddhism, whose role-model was Siddhartha Gautama, born the son of an Indian prince in 563 B.C.E. He renounced a life of wealth and privilege, witnessed the abject despair of deprivation and then rejected worldliness in favor of enlightenment via "the middle way" – between extremes of self-indulgence and self-denial. Buddha is a title meaning "enlightened one," and Siddhartha is said to have attained that status after sitting under a Bodhi tree and vowing never to arise until he found Truth.

Unlike all other major religions of its time, Buddhism saw no need to bring a god into the picture. Its philosophy, embodied in the Four Noble Truths and the Eightfold Path, was a recipe for inner peace and enlightenment. The Buddha himself is regarded as a god-like figure, but adherents believe that anyone can enter into Nirvana and become a Buddha. The most famous Buddhist of our time, not counting actor Richard Gere, is probably the 14th Dalai Lama, who led one sect in Tibet until the government of Communist China exiled him.

Zen Buddhism is a sect that flourished in Japan; it combines aspects of Taoism with Buddhism. Heavy on meditation, Zen maintains that it is useless to use words to describe the Absolute. The goal is to attain satori – enlightenment – through pure intuition, rather than intellect.

Zen and Taoism are do-it-yourself faiths that don't come with requirements to follow a leader – at least, not in their philosophical forms. Sects of both belief systems have developed into religions similar to the structures of Judaism and Christianity, in that they have holy temples and revered leadership hierarchies.

Taoism gave the world the familiar symbol of the yin and yang – a circle divided in two by an S-shaped curve, with one side black and the other white. It symbolizes the inescapable duality of all things. The black side contains a small circle of white, and the white side a small circle of black, indicating that no quality is completely independent of its opposite. Based on the writings of

Lao Tzu from the sixth century B.C.E., Taoism is predominantly mystical. Its adherents seek to become one with the Tao (or "Way"), which is comprised of the primal forces of the universe and everything in it.

Where Christianity has its Jesus, Buddhism its Buddha, and Taoism its Lao Tzu, Confucianism owes its existence to K'ung Fu-tse, whose name is known in the West as Confucius. Many older Americans became familiar with that name from the old Charlie Chan movies, in which the famous Chinese sleuth would often react to situations with a pithy quote, such as, "Confucius say a wise man question himself, a fool others."

Possibly a contemporary of Lao Tzu in ancient China, Confucius coped with his own failed political ambitions by becoming a philosopher who believed that the way to please the gods was through good conduct or Jen (social virtue). Confucius wrote, "What you do not want done to yourself, do not do unto others." A version of that showed up in the New Testament about 600 years later as what we know today as "The Golden Rule."

Religion in dynastic China followed a path similar to that in ancient Egypt – he who sat on the throne made the rules. Confucianism and Taoism vied for supremacy, each taking turns as the state-sanctioned religion while the other was outlawed. By the mid-20th century, Communist China had outlawed both of them in favor of a non-religious cult of personality – Maoism, a reverence for Chinese Communist Party founder Mao Tse-tung.

The newest major religion is Islam, officially born in the year 622 C.E. when Muhammad moved to Yathrib (later renamed Medina) with 70 friends. He formed a tribe of those who accepted him as the Prophet, and he preached the Five Pillars of Islam as the only true path to Heaven.

Muhammad died 10 years later, but his new religion grew into a theocratic empire that stretched from India to Spain over the next 200 years. Today, an estimated 1.3 billion people belong to this religion. "Islam" translates from Arabic into "submission to the will of God," and one who follows this faith is called a Muslim ("one who submits"). Interestingly, the English spelling was

"Moslem" until the late 1980s, when Muslims recommended the new spelling because Moslem was usually pronounced "MAWZ-lem," which sounds too similar to the Arabic word for "oppressor."

Some in the West stereotype Muslims as Third-World terrorists. While this may be understandable, given the atrocities of extremist groups like al-Qaeda (an Arabic term meaning "the base") and Hamas ("zeal"), an entirely different flavor of Islam exists. About 90 percent of the world's Muslims today are from the Sunni sect, which can be generally characterized as conservative and relatively tolerant. The remaining 10 percent tend to be more radical reformers like the Shi'ites and Wahhabis.

Islam bears striking similarities to Christianity and Judaism, and its sacred Qur'an text – which retells many of the same stories found in the Old and New Testaments – identifies the five great early prophets as Adam, Noah, Abraham, Moses and Jesus. We have met some very peaceful Muslims, and we have met some who do not fit that description. You might be able to say the same thing about every religion, and about agnostics and atheists, as well.

The Arabic word "jihad" translates as, "to exert utmost effort; to strive, struggle." It has been interpreted within Islam into a spectrum of meanings ranging from "an inward spiritual struggle to attain perfect faith," all the way to "a political or military struggle to further the Islamic cause."

So we see that while all these religions contain significant differences, they also grew from common roots and retain many similarities. According to the National and World Religion Statistics organization, our planet's population can be classified into belief-system groups of these approximate sizes:

Christianity: 2.1 billion
Islam: 1.3 billion
Secular/nonreligious/agnostic/atheist: 1.1 billion
Hinduism: 900 million
Chinese folk religion (Taoism, Confucianism, etc.): 394 million

Buddhism: 376 million
Primal-indigenous: 300 million
African Traditional & Diasporic: 100 million
Sikhism: 23 million
Juche: 19 million
Spiritism: 15 million
Judaism: 14 million
Baha'i: 7 million
Jainism: 4.2 million
Shinto: 4 million
Cao Dai: 4 million
Zoroastrianism: 2.6 million
Tenrikyo: 2 million
Neo-Paganism: 1 million
Unitarian-Universalism: 800 thousand
Rastafarianism: 600 thousand
Scientology: 500 thousand

We didn't examine many of those faiths on these pages because this is supposed to be simply a chapter on religion, not an entire book. The list itself may be controversial; for instance, is Juche (No. 10) a religion or just the political ideology of North Korea?

You'll also note that Judaism rated a description even though it only ranks 12th on the Top 22. That's because it played an enormous role in spawning the religions that rank No. 1 and No. 2 today.

I'll briefly mention one other religion, simply because it colors my own background, and it's only fair that you understand that. My first belief system was Baha'i Faith, a very new religion founded by a 19th-century Persian exile named Baha'u'llah. Baha'i theology speaks of three interlocking unities: the oneness of God, the oneness of religion, and the oneness of humanity. It's clear to me that my conviction that everything is One stems from my early years in this faith.

The Baha'i believe that religious history is an unfolding process of education planned by God, and that the founders of religions are God's messengers and teachers of this plan. This led to my suspicion that Moses, Jesus, Muhammad, Buddha, Lao Tzu and Baha'u'llah might all have been messengers of truth in their own ways.

But some historians tell us that most of what we read and hear about these "prophets" is legend, not verifiable fact. Moses, Abraham and Lao Tzu might not have existed at all, and the historical record tells us very little about Jesus. Author James Gardner, Ph.D., claims his research establishes that Jesus' real name was Joshua ben Joseph, he wasn't born in Bethlehem, never lived in Nazareth, wasn't born on Dec. 25, his mother wasn't a virgin, his father wasn't a carpenter, and he wasn't crucified.

It doesn't matter. By dictionary definition, religion is a belief system relating to supernatural powers. Faith connotes a transpersonal relationship with God or a higher power. You can follow any one of the Top 22 belief systems listed above, some obscure cult of your own design, or hold no particular spiritual belief system at all and still use the 7 Steps to Wisdom and Inner Peace.

We compare the journey to what you find on the beautiful Greek isle of Santorini; visitors disembark at the small port only to face a challenge if they want to reach the top of the island (and there's little reason to visit Santorini if you aren't going up; otherwise, all you see is a rocky beach). A very steep, switchback trail stands in your way. To reach the top, you can negotiate the stone path on foot, ride a donkey, or take an aerial tram. The hike is fraught with little dangers – uneven rocks, slippery and smelly donkey dung, and physical exhaustion for those less fit. The donkeys come with their own issues – they might bang your legs into walls, stubbornly stop, or even turn around and go back down. And the aerial tram is expensive.

But once you've reached the summit, the experience can be breathtaking. The sheer cliffs, picturesque village and ancient shops rise like a bejeweled crown above the blue sea and surrounding islands. Some believe this was the site of the lost city of Atlantis.

Everyone who makes the journey absorbs this little slice of

heaven in a unique way. They're perceiving the same sights, sounds and smells, yet they color the experience with their own minds. Their method of reaching the top may affect their perceptions, too – did they sweat and strain to achieve this, or merely spend money? Have they dreamed of this moment for years, or is it just one stop on long Mediterranean cruise?

Regardless, they have reached the summit. Whether they got there by walking in Hindu sandals, riding in an atheist tram or clomping up on the back of a Judeo-Christian or Islamic donkey ... they got there. And even though they might all see Nirvana a little differently, they're all standing in the same place.

Religion plays two roles in the 7 Steps to Wisdom and Inner Peace: (1) my belief that we can transcend the material world helped spawn my creation of the 7 Steps, and (2) as you climb this path yourself, the journey will be colored by your own spiritual or atheistic background. But no matter which donkey you ride, the final destination remains the same.

Chapter Eight

ONE MAN'S JOURNEY

If you come to a fork in the road, take it.
Yogi Berra

I am very uncomfortable about this chapter and didn't want to write it, because it focuses on my own story. I told my co-author that this book is not about me; it's about The 7 Steps to Wisdom and Inner Peace. Ultimately, it's about you and your own journey. In fact, any spotlight on oneself runs counter to the guidelines of the 7 Steps. The goal is to remove all ego and self-centeredness from the equation. I am irrelevant.

But my co-author believes that my story will give you perspective. The theory is that if you know some of the events that shaped my life, it will increase my credibility and your understanding. I care nothing about how my credibility appears in the eyes of others – not out of arrogance, but because it simply should have no effect on one's own travels within. However, I appreciate that people won't be inclined to invest the time needed to read a book if they don't think the author knows what he's talking about. And if some knowledge of my background increases your understanding, that's a good thing. But I suppose I have subverted my co-author's wishes by burying this information in Chapter 8 – if you doubted my credibility, why would you keep reading this far? It's the compromise I have struck. I couldn't justify placing this chapter up front.

Disembodied heads, arms, and legs lay scattered amid the bloody torsos. More than 700 bodies of my countrymen lay in a heap on the cement of an outdoor basketball court, rotting in the midday sun. The smell was something I'll never forget. That sight – and thick odor – formed an epiphany in my path to wisdom. Why was this happening? Why were we doing this to ourselves?

It was during the Iran-Iraq War of 1980-88, which we in Iran called the Imposed War. Saddam Hussein's forces had attacked us. It wasn't my war. The Sunni-led Iraq government was trying to conquer Shi'ite-dominated Iran, and I belonged to neither faction. I'd been raised as a Baha'i, and when the Iranian Army learned of my religion, they sent me to the front as a communications officer. They probably figured I'd die, which would help purify the Shi'ite majority, and if I managed to set up a few communications antennae before getting shot, so much the better.

So while I dodged grenades, missiles and mortars, I wasn't just cursing Saddam Hussein, but Iran's Ayatollah Khomeini as well. The pile of twisted human remains on the basketball court left a very deep impact on me because those people all died unnecessarily. It happened after my regiment won a decisive victory. The Iraqis had advanced more than 100 kilometers into Iran, so we launched a surprise counter-attack and captured more than 6,000 Iraqis, gaining back almost all our territory and meeting very little resistance. We thought we had won the war. All these troops had suddenly just surrendered to us. We were celebrating, everyone was getting medals, and for two days, we believed the war was over.

Then Saddam Hussein sent two regiments to attack us from the west. At first, we thought our own troops were shelling us by mistake. My communications team was asked to let them know we weren't the enemy. Just as we were getting ready to transmit data from our front to the command center, I heard a 9-meter missile approaching us. On the battlefield, you can often sense what's coming at you, whether it's a grenade, missile or machine-gun fire. Those 30-foot missiles had hit very close to me three times. They make a distinctive, screaming sound coming in, and we could actually feel this one honing in on us.

The missile struck our antenna and destroyed the mud bunker atop our heads. It also blew apart our truck. This was definitely Iraqi artillery. The war wasn't over, after all. We only had one vehicle left, a Jeep. We piled in and sped off to notify the rest of our regiment.

With the Iraqi army in hot pursuit, we destroyed each bridge after we crossed it. Just as we were trying to break up the last bridge, one of our own tanks and a truck approached.

The soldiers told us they had witnessed a terrible catastrophe. About 750 Iranians had been hit by Iraqi grenades and were pinned down in an area bounded by a mountain on one side and a river on the other. The shelling ceased, but all these people had just one narrow escape route, about 20 feet wide. The Iraqis were closing in, and our Iranians knew they had to get out of there. They decided they would all sneak out slowly and quietly through the tiny pass under the cover of darkness.

But everybody panicked. Tanks rolled over cars, people got trampled and crushed, and of the 750 Iranians, 712 died. They had killed each other in their own frenzy. Senseless. That's what I thought as I stared at all their bodies piled onto the basketball court.

As a communications officer, I roamed the front lines, where the danger level was highest. I narrowly escaped death several times. Once, my communications team and I were driving to a site where we had to erect a wireless antenna. I saw something flying right toward our truck, something that looked like a bullet, a giant bullet. It could have been 10 or 15 miles away, but I had no sense of distance.

I opened the side door and jumped out of the truck, rolling into the mud alongside the road. The truck kept going several feet before the driver finally stopped. War plays tricks with your senses. The big bullet thing came closer, and I could see it was actually a helicopter. It began strafing our truck with machine-gun fire. Hundreds of huge shells smashed into the truck and all around it with thunderous fury. They seemed to be coming from all directions. My driver was a bloody mess. I knew the gunner had seen me jump out of the truck. OK, I thought. I'm next.

The sensation I had was indescribable. Knowing that you're about to die, every cell of your mind and body becomes filled with an intensity of emotion that feels very close to orgasm, strange as that might sound. But the helicopter zoomed past and disappeared into the distance. I heaved a sigh of relief until I saw my driver. He was hit in the neck, shoulder and side. Somehow, he survived. Another time, an Iraqi soldier lobbed a grenade onto my car. It bounced away and exploded, but the force just happened to blast out in a direction away from me.

Three months after I saw all those mutilated bodies on the basketball court, I was finally released from the army, and another man replaced me as communications officer. He was killed seven days later.

The war continued for several more years, but I went home to the apartment I owned in an upscale neighborhood, atop a hill overlooking a king's castle. I came from a family with professional jobs and a better lifestyle than most in Iran. There I struck up a friendship with a very deep and highly educated neighbor who was about to send my life into a completely different direction.

He was a college professor about 15 years my senior, with a Ph.D. in Persian history. We talked about the Iraqi attacks, and he explained the history of warfare between Muslim sects and the continual strife between those who want religion-based government and those who don't. Such wars seem to break out in the Middle East every 40 years or so. My life had been placed in jeopardy by a conflict that had been raging for more than a thousand years, with no resolution in sight.

The professor also gave me a short book about Buddhism, and I found Siddhartha Gautama's story fascinating. Here was a man who had every possible material comfort – he was the son of a king – yet he gave it all up to walk into the wilderness and search for truth. Why would he leave that comfortable life?

It was perhaps not unlike the life I had enjoyed. All my material needs were satisfied. But my country seemed to be in a state of upheaval, and as a non-Muslim, I felt torn as to which path to follow. My sister and brothers were thrown out of their jobs because they were of Baha'i Faith. The new government said all non-Muslims had a choice – convert or die. In some cases, they would literally put a gun to your head and demand that you say you're a Muslim. If you refuse, they pull the trigger. Photos of this persuasive method ran in the newspapers so all non-Muslims would get the point.

The professor and I spent many hours in conversation – history, philosophy, religion, science – and he knew I was a seeker. "I think you need to go to India," he told me one day. "I have a friend who studied with me at the university in Germany. He's a Hindu, now living in Kolkata. I can send you to him."

"Why?" It is the question I've always asked about everything.

"I think you need to experience Hindu philosophy a bit. It's very close to what you think you want to accomplish."

That was good enough for me. Leaving Iran was very difficult at the time. Nobody trusted anybody else. But another friend was able to get a visa for me, so I locked my apartment door and left the key with the professor. "I might come back," I said. "Or I might not."

I stuffed cash into tubes, stashed them in my backpack and set out for India. I landed in Pune, where I decided to wander like the Buddha, following my instincts and just absorbing the people and the culture.

One morning at a café I frequented for breakfast, I encountered an intriguing, solitary young man in orange robes. The café owner gave him free tea and something to eat, and I wondered why. The young man and I began to talk. In very poor English (our only common language), he told me about his life, his beliefs and his religion. Begging for sustenance was part of his faith, and his countrymen accepted and supported it – sort of like a Christian preacher being supported by his congregation. This robed man focused entirely on metaphysical and philosophical pursuits, and I became transfixed. When he finished his meal, he rose.

"I have to go," he said.

"I'm going with you."

"What?" He looked confused.

"Wherever you're going, I'm going."

I made it clear that I wanted to learn from him, and he agreed to let me tag along. We walked for hours, passing through several villages until we finally came to a strange-looking temple. Inside, I could see something moving; something with two horns. I felt a little stab of fear but followed him inside anyway. The beast with horns was a goat.

I now know that animal sacrifice is still practiced in parts of India, and goats are beheaded with a single stroke on Tuesdays and Saturdays. But all I knew about this particular sect was that the man prayed and slept in a small cave at the temple, and he kept a goat there. I walked and talked with him until noon the next day, then started to travel alone, throughout India, in hopes of gaining insight into the people and their beliefs.

One early lesson was why Hindus eat such spicy food – the spicier, the better. They believe it invigorates their spirit by deadening their senses. Sharp senses can distract one from inner truth, so spicy-hot food like peppers can help them reach a higher level of spirituality. This belief is more common in southern India than the north, where spicy food is thought to cause unhappiness, sorrow and disease.

In the coastal state of Goa, I found God ... or at least, a person who claimed he was God. The region of Goa is a melting pot of races, religions and cultures. It's also known for beautiful beaches and free-spirited lawlessness. On a pristine, white-sand beach in Goa, I encountered a Persian fellow who said his name was Iraj, and oh by the way, he also happened to be God. He seemed to have a logical, acceptable answer for every question I asked, and I found him fascinating. He may or may not have been God, but he seemed highly evolved. He was beyond accomplishing anything. He just seemed like he was already THERE.

I asked if I could come with him and do whatever it was that he was doing. So we walked and talked for a while, and I felt like I was stepping ever closer to what I was seeking – wisdom and inner peace. Later we met another seeker, a young man from France who was learning to play the Indian drum.

"*Mon ami*, what you are doing is *magnifique*," he said. "*Si vous plait*, I would come with you."

So the three of us lived for a while in a New Delhi tourist camp for foreigners. We paid $1 a night for a 5x10-foot room, where we supplied our own bedrolls. There we met a jovial fellow from Scotland who would buy cheap watches for a buck or two, then approach tourists in New Delhi and say he was desperate for money, and would they be interested in buying his watch for $30? He did that every day.

Eventually, our group of drifters and grifters ended up in Katmandu, where we met a Hindu from an upper-caste family. We visited his temple – not for food or shelter, although we certainly needed them – but to learn. The Hindu found us interesting, and we were fascinated by his devotion, his philosophy and his religion. Soon we surrendered ourselves into the service of the temple. That led to the experience I mentioned in the Introduction, when I was told to drink a concoction made with cobra venom so I could "die" and be born anew.

I've already mentioned my encounter with Bhagwan Shree Rajneesh, who started his movement in Pune and eventually took it to the United States. Despite the controversy that dogged him throughout his final years, Rajneesh was a brilliant man. He earned a masters degree in philosophy from the University of Saugar and taught philosophy at the University of Jabalpur for nine years. When I met with him, Rajneesh's intent seemed pure, and his mind clear and focused.

"If we cannot create the 'new man' in the coming 20 years, then humanity has no future," Rajneesh said. "The holocaust of a global suicide can only be avoided if a new kind of man can be created."

While his timeline and perhaps even his predicted consequences might be questioned, I still believe he was basically right – our future hinges on our ability to change. In 1984, I left India for the U.S., but not to follow Rajneesh. He settled in Oregon, where his "Rajneeshees" organization wobbled toward lawlessness. In my opinion, the movement became corrupted by greed. Rajneesh is said to have lived in luxury and owned more than 100 cars, including 27 Rolls-Royces ... not exactly the "middle way" that the Buddha recommended.

I settled in Southern California, because my future wife, Mona, was planning to enroll at UCLA. We'd met in Iran before the war, and wherever my journey would take me, I knew I wanted her to be part of it.

So my path toward wisdom and inner peace – not *the* path, just one path – carried me through wealth, poverty, faith, loss of faith, war, death, education, the company of gurus, enlightenment, travel, love and eventually a family.

In the ensuing years, my continuing studies and meditations have led me to formulate the hypothesis I now call The 7 Steps to Wisdom and Inner Peace, which you are about to learn. I know this path works because I have experienced it. I've felt the calm neutrality and Oneness of Step 7. Am I a master who lives in this state of bliss all the time? I don't know if anybody does, because we still have to interact with the material world if we want to earn a living, raise a family and pay the bills.

But I believe it has been done. The 13th Century Persian mystic and poet Rumi seems to have been there throughout his final years. Rumi lived, wrote and spoke in a way that was neither exclusively Sufi, nor Hindu, nor Jewish, nor Christian. He appeared as our highest possible state of existence – a fully evolved human, not bound by cultural or physical limitations. Even today, his life and work touches everyone who learns of it.

A person who lives in Step 7 has completely transcended wanting, receiving, giving, balance and satisfaction. He has detached from all worldly concerns and accepted death. He spends time in Nirvana, Shangri-la, Heaven, Absolute Bliss Consciousness ... a person like that has no need to name it or write a book about it.

While I have experienced Step 7 and will do so again, I spend much of my time in a more temporal state, and therefore I'm motivated to take all these concepts in my head and all my journal writings in Farsi and crystallize them into an English text.

My decision to write comes from a desire to share with you. I realize that a person existing solely in Step 7 no longer experiences desires, so there may come a time when I don't care about this book anymore. And neither will you. We'll simply be *there* all the time, at one with the Absolute. It warms me just thinking about it. So let's take a look at that road map.

Chapter Nine

THE 7 STEPS

One's first step in wisdom is to question everything –
and one's last is to come to terms with everything.
Georg C. Lichtenberg

Why, you may ask, are there exactly seven steps to wisdom and inner peace? Why not three or 19 or 121? Is our number merely arbitrary? And if so, what validity could it possibly have?

There are seven steps because that's how many turning points I personally experienced as I traveled a path guided by everything in my world – which included all the religious, scientific and philosophical influences previously mentioned.

Perhaps "turning points" would have been a better description, but "step" is simpler. I wrote about them extensively in my Farsi journals, and since then, I've studied and analyzed each one.

My own journey took me through seven very distinct, major transformations, which sometimes felt like breaking points, although that description sounds a bit harsh. You could call them pathways, transitions or keys, but I picture them as significant stair steps leading upward. We'll examine each in detail during the next seven chapters.

You may encounter lots of smaller stops along the way that bring you closer to your goal, but those are more like growth spurts. The real change that occurs from step to step is more on the order of a transformation. You become a completely different human being.

Maybe it's no coincidence that the number of steps ended up being seven, which is somewhat magical in its own right. It's a prime number (evenly divisible only by 1 and itself), and seven is deeply embedded in nature and the mind of mankind. We have seven days in a week, seven wonders of the world, seven seas, seven deadly sins, seven daughters of Atlas in the Pleiades, the seven ages of man, seven levels of Hell, seven prismatic colors, and seven notes on the musical scale. In nuclear physics, there are only seven different numbers of nucleons that can be arranged into complete shells within an atomic nucleus.

George Miller wrote an oft-quoted article in 1956 which established that the average person's short-term memory can effectively handle just seven elements. Today, some of the more savvy software companies design their pull-down menus around this theory, limiting the user's choices to just seven options. "Perhaps there is something deep and profound behind all these sevens, something just calling out for us to discover it," Miller wrote. "But I suspect that it is only a pernicious, Pythagorean coincidence."

Ultimately, the magic-number theory is irrelevant to me. If I had experienced 19 steps to wisdom and inner peace, I would have written about all 19. I experienced seven. And here they are, in quick brush strokes (the deeper detail comes in the subsequent chapters on each step):

1. Wanting: We are born with wants, and for most of us, this primal urge never goes away. We want food. Warmth. Protection. Love. Toys. The wants continue to grow and evolve, and few people ever feel like all their wants are fully satisfied. Even the very rich still have desires that wealth can't fulfill. Everyone's journey begins with this step. Unless you can move beyond wanting, you'll never achieve inner peace.

2. Receiving: Everybody moves into this step immediately after wanting, but it's not nearly as primitive an experience. Wanting is a basic instinct that feels about the same at age 98 as it did at age 1 month. But receiving begins with sensations like a mother's touch and becomes something very different by the time you learn to receive the scent of a rose, the feel of fine silk or the sounds of Mozart's Symphony No. 40 in G Minor. We develop our abilities to receive in order to fill the holes we perceive in ourselves.

3. Giving: Many see giving as self-sacrifice, but it really starts as a selfish act and, in many ways, remains so our entire lives. A baby quickly learns that its desires will be satisfied if it "gives" something – first it gives the wail of crying, which is certainly not a welcome gift to the parent, but usually results in a desire being satisfied. Eventually the individual learns to give smiles, kisses, good grades, hard work, love and charitable contributions. In return, the individual gets food, parental protection, approval, money, love and tax deductions. Love, as a facet of Giving, moves you closer to Balance.

4. Balance: This is the middle step, the fulcrum of all seven. An altered state of consciousness is required to achieve real balance, and meditation is a safe and productive method. We often feel a sense of balance when we experience love. Our emotions fill us with pleasure. We want, receive and give all at the same time. The world seems right ... balanced. But as anyone who has ever been in love can tell you, it's not perfect. Pain is still part of the equation. If not, we wouldn't have country songs.

5. Satisfaction: This occurs when, thanks to wisdom born of your mystical experience, you finally break free from wanting. What you have is enough, and you don't want anymore. You exist in your own universe, and you don't need anybody else's universe. You have left the material world and moved into the spiritual. You'll never be unhappy again. Let us repeat that, because we doubt that you can believe it right now: You will never be unhappy again. And it gets even better than that.

6. Detachment: Few people ever reach this stage. It occurs when you recognize that you are two beings, one physical and the other spiritual. By detaching from the physical, you free yourself. While you still attend to your bodily needs, you live in another world. You see without seeing, feel without touching. You gain a level of understanding that transcends words and teaching. Materialistic people (almost everybody) will misunderstand and reject you, but you won't care, because you have detached from what matters to them.

7. Oneness: This step can be envisioned as the death of your former self. It's an existence where you can live within the realm of the Absolute at will. Your spiritual existence has rejoined its source, just as it will when your physical body dies. Those who have been here while their bodies were still breathing generally live in Step 7 for periods of time, then return to the stage of Detachment or even Satisfaction for the purpose of interacting with the physical world.

You'll notice that the seven steps are balanced – three on the physical side, three on the spiritual, and one in the middle which is itself called "Balance."

This is just a brief taste of what awaits you. Reading these short descriptions doesn't complete your journey. We've only just begun.

Chapter Ten

WANTING

Be careful what you set your heart upon
- for it will surely be yours.
James Baldwin

Right now, my mind feels like it's racing in a hundred different directions. What do I need to say in this chapter, and how do I want to say it? Will readers understand concepts that transcend their five senses? What did my wife tell me to pick up at the store on the way home? The car needs gas. Where can I find the cheapest gas? Hey, did that guy just pass gas?

That's how most of us exist at any given moment. But a newborn baby is completely different. She has just one all-consuming focus: wanting. She sleeps about 17 hours a day and spends most of her few waking hours in a state of wanting. She wants to be fed. She wants to be warm. She wants to be held. A baby knows nothing but primal desires. Instinctively, she communicates by crying, and the communication holds just one meaning: "I want."

If the baby is unfortunate enough to have first-time parents, her cries may confuse and worry Mom and Dad.

"What does she want?"

"I don't know. I just fed her. Maybe she needs to be changed."

"No, you idiots," the baby thinks. "Crying means pain, fear, discomfort or loneliness. Pick one. It's a simple process of elimination. Didn't they teach you anything?"

We're kidding, of course. The baby is thinking no such thing because she is a Zen Master. She has the amazing ability to focus every cell of her body on just one thought: "I want." Nothing else enters her picture.

Within the first few weeks, the baby's weak eyes start to focus on objects, like her mother's face, and people wave colorful objects in front of her and make silly noises with their mouths. Her eyes follow the movements. She grows curious. But her focus remains singular: "I want." Only now, instead of wanting just to be fed or held, she wants something more. She wants to satisfy her curiosity. Babies naturally become curious about everything. They want ... to know. Soon – say, when she turns 15 – she will also want to have and the older she gets, the more she will want to have, but that's not my point. My point is that the most primitive drive is Wanting. And that's Step 1 on your path toward wisdom and inner peace.

Congratulations. You already reached Step 1. Actually, congratulations aren't in order until you move past Step 1, because Wanting comes as standard equipment. You had it the minute you rolled off the assembly line. Later, you'll want to order the special options.

Before our tone becomes too flippant, we want to examine some important points about your own personal journey. First, it's safe to assume you still bear at least some elements of this primal Wanting stage in your internal makeup. If you are reading a book that promises 7 Steps to Wisdom and Inner Peace, you want those qualities, or you at least want to explore the possibilities.

But your Wanting has matured to a very different and distorted level from the newborn baby. Her wants are limited to simple needs – food and comfort. Her neocortex isn't even part of the process; indeed, that complex portion of the brain responsible for conscious thought, spatial reasoning and sensory perception isn't fully wired yet. Conversely, your wants are influenced by so many outside forces that even a clinical psychiatrist could only guess at their roots and consequences.

Let's go back to the illustration of an infant. At some point, she learns that whenever she makes certain noises and facial expressions, she gets positive feedback from Mom and Dad. This leads to the care and attention she wants. So, while Mom and Dad listen to the coos and goos and admire her little smiles, they feel stirrings of love for this cute and helpless little girl – never realizing that she is simply manipulating them, in a non-cognitive way, into satisfying her wants.

When all her wants are fully satisfied, she has achieved all the wisdom and inner peace she needs at this point. She is One with the Absolute. Blissful. Hence the term, "sleeping like a baby."

The baby owns another advantage over you: she knows what she wants. Her desires are simple, and she has no confusion over them. She's like Audrey II, the man-eating plant in the stage musical "The Little Shop of Horrors" who screams, "Feed me!"

Once fed, she remains blissful ... until another want arises. Contrast this to the typical adult mind, which is filled with self-destructive and conflicting wants that usually didn't even originate with the individual who is now haunted by them. Let's say you want to be a surgeon. Your parents always told you that you could be a great brain surgeon, and you studied hard, got into medical school, then struggled and began to question yourself. You start to feel miserable and fear you won't be able to get what you want, and you will only disappoint your parents.

You really want to be a surgeon. At least, that's what you keep telling yourself. Deep down inside, you really love playing the clarinet, and you're very gifted at it, but how are you going to make a decent living? Playing on the street corner with an upside-down hat on the sidewalk in front of you? No, you really want to be a surgeon. You need to be a surgeon. Anything less would be failure.

Sometimes our "wants" can be planted inside us by foreign sources, and we allow them to grow in our minds like cancers. We believe they're truly our own wants, but they're not. Often, it's more difficult to know what you want than it is to get it. We can only envy the infant who knows with such clarity.

Just think of all the desires that invade our psyches throughout our lives. We want good grades so we can get into a good college, and we want a degree so we can get a good job. We want a good job so we can earn a good salary. We want a pretty wife to satisfy our sexual drive or a wealthy husband for security. We want a hot car and a big house to prove our worth to others. We want our children to be high achievers so they will succeed in life. It goes on and on.

Every one of those desires mentioned above is artificial. They're all created by other people's perceptions – not yours. Whether you realize it or not, they were taught to you in a manner not unlike indoctrination. And as long as you chase them, you will never be free.

The Zen Master baby is curious about everything, and so were you, once upon a time. Now you're frustrated, bored or both. What happened? Did you learn everything there is to learn? No, you've just undergone brain surgery, performed by society.

When the "want" was pure wisdom, your path was genuine. When it became artificial things like grades, degrees and money, you lost your drive, because you knew intuitively that something had gone terribly wrong. Even those who achieve all the outward signs of success feel an emptiness deep inside. Unable to touch that emptiness or identify it, they try to drown it with alcohol or sex or gluttony or fast cars or big houses or maybe even religion, but the only thing they're truly certain about is that something's still missing from their lives.

In order to make our point, our words may sometimes appear harsh or accusatory. So allow us to clarify: we're not suggesting there's anything wrong with you, or that you should or must change. And while our words may help point you in a more fulfilling direction, your ultimate guide and guru will always be yourself. Once the energies inside you begin to re-align, you'll become self-propelled. We're just explaining reality as we and many others have experienced it. This is our picture; you will know when you find your own.

Maybe you're stuck believing you're an apple when you're really an orange. Once you accept and understand yourself and find your true center, you embark on the path to inner peace. It's the same principle espoused by Hippocrates, the father of modern medicine: "The natural healing force within us," he said, "is the greatest force in getting well." In the same manner, if you remove the conditioning and blockages with which society has burdened you, your spiritual being will naturally heal itself and seek to return to its source. You will become like the baby Zen Master ... in its blissful stage, not its wanting stage.

The secret to moving past the primal stage of wanting is to stop wanting, or, as spiritual author Guy Finley says, to want what life wants. In this case, "life" can be envisioned as God, the Tao, the quantum potential force, or simply life.

Wanting only what you want is a recipe for unhappiness and frustration. You form attachments to desires that aren't always within your control. Wanting "what life wants" – which is another way of saying what life brings you – is a pathway to serenity. This philosophy of acceptance is captured in the first verse of the Serenity Prayer by Reinhold Niebuhr:

God, grant me the serenity
to accept the things I cannot change;
Courage to change the things I can;
And wisdom to know the difference.

Finley writes in "The Secret of Letting Go" that the following will result when you want only what you want:

1. You are often nervous and anxious because life may not cooperate with your plans.
2. You are willing to sacrifice whatever it takes to get what you want, and this may include your integrity.
3. You are usually scheming in some way to win your next victory.
4. You are either in a battle or recovering from one.
5. You are unable to rest quietly when you need to.
6. You are easily angered when someone or something gets in your way.
7. You are forever driven to want something else.
8. You are against anyone else who also wants what you want.
9. You are certain that what you have is who you are.
10. You are always trying to convince yourself that you got

what you wanted.

Now carefully consider what happens when you want what life wants:

1. You are never disappointed with what happens.
2. You are always in the right place at the right time.
3. You are quietly confident no matter what the circumstances.
4. You are out of the reach of anger and anxiety.
5. You are awake and sensitive to your surroundings.
6. You are free of ever feeling as though you've missed out.
7. You are never thrown for a loss.
8. You are in total command of events.
9. You are mentally quiet.
10. You are eternally grateful.

These are concepts easily accepted by those comfortable with Eastern philosophies, but the Western mind may stumble here. Americans in particular value a "can-do" attitude that respects the individual who changes the world to fit his desires. The Oakland Raiders pro football team has an unofficial slogan to match: "We don't take what the defense gives us, we take what we want." It's no coincidence that their logo shows a pirate's face and crossed swords.

It's also no coincidence that the U.S., despite spending more per capita on medical care than any nation in the world, ranks No.1 in mental illness, heart disease and hypertension, and has a worse mortality rate than 18 other nations.

Common sense tells you that wisdom and inner peace will lead to happier, healthier lives. Statistics show that the Western mind desperately needs this wisdom and inner peace. Yet this nation is still stuck in the vicious cycle of artificial desires.

"You mean, I won't be happy even if I get everything I want?" No, you won't be happy. You'll be stuck on the level discussed in the next chapter – Receiving.

Chapter Eleven

RECEIVING

Life is not a having and a getting, but a being and a becoming.
Myrna Loy

You can't always get what you want, but if you try sometimes, you just might find you get what you need. At least, that's what Mick Jagger and Keith Richards sang, and they studied in the Rishikesh tents of the Maharishi Mahesh Yogi, so we might assume they learned a thing or two about Enlightenment.

Their song rings of philosophical depth, and it seems to speak to the keys for getting past Step 1: if you only want what *life* wants, rather than what *you* want, you'll never be disappointed. You get what you need. But the Rolling Stones' song loses all mysticism when you discover its true genesis: Before a 1968 concert in Muncie, Indiana, Mick and Keith stopped by Brown's Pharmacy and Soda Fountain, and Mick ordered a Cherry Coke. John Birkemeier, a college student working the counter, said they didn't have Cherry Coke. Mick couldn't believe it. Birkemeier calmly told the rock superstar, "You can't always get what you want." Mick and Keith wrote the song and recorded it a few months later, including the line, "We decided that we would have a soda ... My favorite flavor, cherry red." Philosophical depth lies wherever you find it.

Like Mick Jagger, you might be able to understand the futility of the "Receiving" stage by not getting what you want, but a far more effective lesson is taught when you *do* get what you want. Maybe something like this has happened to you: when I was a small boy, I saw a toy that I desperately wanted. I asked my parents to buy it for me, I dreamed about playing with it, and I talked about it constantly. It became an obsession.

Then one day, my parents surprised me with a gift – the very toy I coveted. My whole world was perfect, birds sang in the skies, the sun was shining on me, there *was* a God. I was thrilled – for about two days. Then I realized the toy was too big and bulky, I didn't know what to do with it, and playing with it wasn't fun. I put it away and never played with it again. Wanting leads to receiving, but any happiness that comes from receiving is artificial and necessarily short-lived.

As Neil Sedaka sang in "The Hungry Years," the "things that we were after were much better from afar ... We climbed the ladder leading us nowhere ... two of us together, building castles in the air."

The step of Receiving is the time you spend building castles in the air. Eventually, when you move past the step of Receiving, you'll realize all that time and energy were spent on frivolous pursuits. Even if you could have everything you thought you ever wanted, you would not be fulfilled. Enlightenment isn't about having "things."

Most of the known universe seems to exist in a flux between the Wanting and Receiving stages. Even non-living matter can be animated by these primitive drives; no consciousness required.

An electron "wants" to exist in its most stable state, but if it collides with an "excited" atom and absorbs a photon, the electron will jump into a state of higher energy and a new orbit. Soon the electron will spontaneously emit a photon packet – a quantum – to release its new energy, thereby jumping back (the so-called quantum leap) to a different orbit in a more stable state. A mindless, single-celled amoeba moves toward edible algae while avoiding particles that aren't suitable for food. A lizard needs to eat, so it catches an ant, and it feels satisfied until hunger creates another desire. You want a new car, so you buy the best you can afford, and you're happy – until you see a better one and start to feel that gnawing feeling of "want" again.

All these entities are cycling back and forth between Wanting and Receiving. It dominates their existence. But there's a big difference between human desires and the yin-and-yang existence of the so-called lower energy forms like electrons, amoebas and lizards. Wanting and Receiving might be all those lower forms require to remain in balance with the Absolute. Lizards don't want more than they need. A lion doesn't kill every antelope and zebra in its territory. They live in balance with nature. Only humans kill because of artificial or imagined desires. Only humans need guidance in how to move past this cycle of Wanting and Receiving.

So here is the secret to breaking out of this recursive pattern: you must place no importance on either one. You have to accept that Wanting and Receiving – beyond the basic survival instincts – are ultimately meaningless. If you can't accomplish this, you will spend the rest of your life locked in a continuous cycle of Wanting and Receiving, never to experience true wisdom and inner peace. You'll live in a state of alienation, always striving to prove something or have something. Other people with similar desires (and that includes almost everybody) will become your enemies, at least on a subliminal level. True happiness will be impossible.

The Katha Upanishad says the bridge to spiritual realization is as thin and sharp as a razor's edge. It's far easier to fall onto either side than it is to follow the path. Imagine yourself walking this razor's edge, with Wanting on one side and Receiving on the other. The secret to successfully negotiating this impossibly narrow path is simply to *be*. No Wanting, no Receiving, just being. Then the temptations of Wanting and Receiving disappear.

It requires you to see without judgment. Whatever is, simply *is*. You don't label the juicy steak "good" and the coyote that eats your cat "bad." All things are what they are. They have substance or causes and effects, they can be understood to some degree, but everything is part of nature, including all manmade objects and activities. (After all, are we not natural beings, too?) If you can avoid assigning absolute values to things, you can avoid the potential pitfalls of Wanting and Receiving.

This undoubtedly is a very alien concept for Western minds. You've probably spent your entire life passing judgment on everything and everybody. Indeed, your formal education has taught you to do just that. Coloring outside the lines was bad, standing in line was good. The Holocaust was bad, the bombing of Hiroshima was good.

Your own worthiness was judged by the teachers who assigned you a letter grade from A to F. That's all you amounted to – somebody else's choice of a letter. I'm not suggesting that the opposites of my preceding examples are true; the bombing of Hiroshima wasn't *bad*, and the Holocaust wasn't *good*. They were both just natural events, little different from Hurricane Katrina. The fact that humans caused those other events is irrelevant, because humans are as natural as the wind. The enlightened reaction to all events is: "What can I learn from this? What can I take from this that will help me remain balanced and One with the Absolute?" It might mean planning in advance for a hurricane, or devising ways to stop aggression.

A man living in balanced wisdom and inner peace doesn't just sit on a log contemplating his navel. He can be a proactive force for progress, but his definition of progress might be different from yours. Western-style or American progress means bigger, faster, stronger, easier or brighter, but the balanced individual doesn't equate those terms with "good." To the enlightened, progress simply means moving toward balance.

Even the act of moving toward balance need not be judged as good; it's simply the natural order of all things. You begin to move toward perfect balance when you succeed in dismissing Wanting and Receiving as unimportant. That balance enables you to cross the razor-thin bridge with ease.

A good yardstick for measuring where you are with regard to Receiving is the way you accept praise and compliments. How do you feel when someone praises you? Proud? Gratified? Embarrassed? Unworthy? None of those reactions can be found on the path to Enlightenment. A being who has achieved wisdom and inner peace would react with indifference.

Research by the Gallup organization indicates that 69 percent of workers in American business would rather get positive feedback and recognition from their bosses than anything else, including a pay raise. That means they are still stuck here in Step 2, Receiving. They have difficulty feeling good about themselves unless they receive something. Even if their self-esteem is high, they like to receive praise simply because it makes them feel better about themselves, so they're still stuck on Receiving.

We're not suggesting that everyone's top priority should instead be the pay raise. We're saying that *all* receiving should be irrelevant, whether it's money, praise or anything else. Maybe "neutral" is a better word than irrelevant, because the person who moves past Step 2 is no longer motivated by Wanting and therefore is no longer gratified by Receiving.

Meeting your survival necessities will always remain a basic instinct; you need food, water and shelter. Earning money will enable you to satisfy those needs. But you will seek a livelihood that fosters balance in your life, rather than take a job you hate just so you can have enough money to feed your insatiable desire to Receive.

You'll know you've finally transcended Step 2 when Receiving means absolutely nothing to you. Self-esteem will mean nothing. Ego will be non-existent, because you'll realize there is no "you" that's separate from all the rest. "We're all one, and life flows on within you and without you" (George Harrison).

The myth of individuality seems to be supported by strong evidence. More than 6 billion people inhabit this planet, and structurally, not one is exactly like you. No two humans can share the same DNA except identical twins and clones, and even those "carbon copies" will bear differences. The cliché about how "they broke the mold when they made you" is true. There has never been another organism exactly like you, and there never will be ever again.

Yet at the same time, your "uniqueness" isn't separate and distinct from the whole. The feeling that you are an individual is an illusion. The Hindu word "Maya" has many different shades of meaning, but it is most often used to describe the cosmic illusion that makes the One appear to us as a multiplicity.

This illusion – that we are all separate beings – hides the deep spiritual truth of the Absolute. We are all just tiny expressions of a single One, and you are not your DNA. You will accept this intuitively when you attend a funeral and gaze upon the deceased. The DNA is still there, lying in front of you. The skin bag and all its contents have not yet ceased to exist. But the essence of the being that inhabited that skin bag has gone back to its source. You can feel the truth of it just by looking at the body.

Some believe The Beatles' song "I Am the Walrus" was just a bunch of nonsense lyrics or maybe fanciful clues to the mystery of how Paul McCartney "died," but it actually started with a line that describes our ultimate oneness: "I am he, as you are he, as you are me, and we are all together." When acceptance of this truth fills every cell of your body, you will begin to release your attachment to Receiving. As one gradually loses that preoccupation, the natural progression is to explore Giving.

Chapter Twelve

GIVING

The love we give away is the only love we keep.
Elbert Hubbard

You are now entering the final step of the material world. Understand the step of Giving, then transcend it, and you will move into the spiritual realm. Giving takes you beyond the selfish and primitive acts of Wanting and Receiving, but beware. The road is filled with potholes. Giving can easily drag you back into those old, familiar traps.

The act of giving is often portrayed as altruistic: "Giving, in its purest form, expects nothing in return" (Beth Polson). Certainly, you already know that's seldom true in the real world. Most people give only because they expect it will lead to receiving. It's an expectation that dates back to Biblical times and was sanctified in the New Testament. "Give and it shall be given unto you; good measure, pressed down, and shaken together, and running over, shall men give unto your bosom." (Luke 6:38).

Whether you're giving money, property, favors or love, chances are that you expect, or at least hope, that your kindness will be returned in some measurable and concrete way.

The Book of Proverbs says, "A generous man will prosper; he who refreshes others will himself be refreshed." The Book of Matthew says that your giving should "be in secret. Then your Father, who sees what is done in secret, will reward you."

It's all about the reward! Giving plunges us right back into Wanting and Receiving.

But despair not, because there's no denying that the mere act of giving is a step forward. You're not ALWAYS thinking of yourself anymore. You've learned that sharing and giving can foster harmony in the world around you, and that's good for everybody.

Sometimes, the only benefit you get from Giving is the sense of self-satisfaction that you performed an honorable act and someone else's life is better for it. You've likely heard of the "Anonymous Acts of Kindness" movement, wherein you are encouraged to perform such selfless actions as paying the road toll for the car behind you or secretly mowing your neighbor's lawn. The feeling that that kind of charity gives you is a reward in itself ... certainly a more elevated reward, but still a reward. The altruism looks a bit blurry, because your ego is still involved.

Recall the scene in the movie "Field of Dreams," after the Ray Kinsella character (Kevin Costner) carves a baseball diamond out of his cornfield and watches as others use his field to realize their fantastic dreams.

"I did it all," Ray says in agitation. "I listened to the voices, I did what they told me, and not once did I ask what's in it for me."

"What are you saying, Ray?" the ballplayer Shoeless Joe Jackson replies calmly.

"I'm saying, uh ... what's in it for me?"

In the end, there *was* something in it for Ray. He got to reconnect with his long-dead father, in the guise of a spirit baseball player. Popular fiction plays into our human instincts. We believe there *should* be something in it for Ray.

Just now, you might be coming to realize that you and almost everyone around you have already spent time in each of the first three steps to wisdom and inner peace. We all recognize Wanting on a primal level, and we have all experienced how Wanting leads to Receiving. Even Giving comes naturally, as when a small child gives hugs in order to reinforce her sense of parental security.

At some point during our childhood, we are taught about other kinds of giving, and soon the act doesn't seem to come quite so easily. So far, it's the only step that requires some inner work. A child can grasp the concept of giving a birthday present, yet still feel a twinge of jealousy when the birthday girl gets a toy that the child wants for herself. Did we say a twinge? We've seen some children cry, scream and actually try to steal presents from the birthday girl.

Some of us never quite outgrow that stage; we've also heard

grown women complain they didn't receive nearly as nice a gift from Mrs. So-and-So as the one they gave her. And men who loan their tools to a neighbor might grouse if that neighbor isn't equally generous in loaning his DVDs.

So how do you progress past this kind of two-faced Giving? You do it by accepting the truth that your wisdom and inner peace will come only after you place no importance whatsoever on Having, Wanting OR Giving. That's right, all three steps must be left behind.

The first two are relatively easy. A good folk song or self-help book can show us the folly of greed (Charles Dickens' "A Christmas Carol" is also a good dramatization of the moral), but how does one justify a lack of attention to Giving? Isn't that supposed to be a good trait? In most cultures, the answer is yes. But that's the problem. The idea that Giving is good comes from human culture. It's not organic to our species or the universe, but instead more of an artificial construct.

The only natural mission of everything in the universe is to become balanced. That's the only organic driving force. Everything else is artificial. Beyond our basic need for food, water, shelter and procreation, there is no amount of Wanting, Having or Giving that will foster greater balance. This doesn't mean you shouldn't live in a nicer house than you need, or that you shouldn't help your fellow men and women. It only means that if you wish to achieve wisdom and inner peace, the acts of Having, Receiving and Giving must be irrelevant to you. If, in the process of pursuing your bliss through greater balance, you acquire fortune and fame and can give much to charity, fine. But don't hold those ends as goals.

While we have all spent time as slaves to the first three steps during various periods of our lives, we can only move past them when we accept that they have no bearing on our goal to achieve Oneness. Time and energy spent on Wanting more, Receiving more and Giving more is just time and energy wasted. It throws you in the opposite direction of balance.

We must address another key element of Giving, however, which is far more complex than those just discussed. Let's talk about love.

Love is Giving, Wanting and Receiving all rolled into one. It taps into parts of our brain designed for procreation and survival of the species, but as any poet can tell you, love seems like so much more than that. When we talk about wisdom and inner peace, there's no avoiding the question, "What's love got to do with it?"

Love brings us closer to the next step (Balance) because it elevates us from pure selfishness into a realm of fuzzy oneness with the world around us, a temporary euphoria. It's fuzzy and temporary because romantic love appears to be little more than a chemical reaction in the brain that soon fades. But it's an important step forward, nonetheless.

In "The Art of Loving," Erich Fromm writes that love is about unity, not conformity; oneness, not sameness; openness, not isolation; togetherness, not separation; activity, not passivity.

"They are starved for it," Fromm writes. "They watch endless numbers of films about happy and unhappy love stories, they listen to hundreds of trashy songs about love — yet hardly anyone thinks that there is anything that needs to be learned about love."

Or maybe love seems like such a mystery to people that "learning about love" seems fruitless. Many view love as they view great art; they don't quite know how to define it, but "I'll know it when I see it."

Love is the first transcendental experience of our lives. It carries us to a place beyond words. In the movie "Don Juan DeMarco," the title character played by Johnny Depp says to his psychiatrist, "There are only four questions of value in life, Don Octavio: What is sacred? Of what is the spirit made? What is worth living for? And what is worth dying for? The answer to each is the same: only love."

Our poetic, lyrical and prose words about love could, and do, fill libraries. We are fascinated by this emotion that defies description and yet has been described endlessly. Writer and orator Robert G. Ingersoll (1833-1899) wrote:

Love is the only bow on life's dark cloud.
It is the Morning and the Evening Star.
It shines upon the cradle of the babe,
and sheds its radiance upon the quiet tomb.
It is the mother of Art,
inspirer of poet, patriot, and philosopher.
It is the air and light of every heart, builder of every home,
kindler of every fire on every hearth.
It was the first to dream of immortality.
It fills the world with melody,
for Music is the voice of Love.
Love is the magician, the enchanter,
that changes worthless things to joy,
and makes right royal kings and queens of common clay.
It is the perfume of the wondrous flower – the heart,
and without that sacred passion, that divine swoon,
we are less than beasts;
but with it, earth is heaven
and we are gods.

Not everyone approaches love with such starry-eyed reverence, of course. Writer Ambrose Bierce (1842-1914) defined love as "a temporary insanity, curable by marriage." Most lovers probably side with Blaise Pascal (1623-1662), who said, "The heart has its reasons which reason knows not of." He thereby allows for the mystery of love to remain.

What's fascinating about Pascal's quote is that, as a mathematician and physicist, this 17th Century scientist seemed to concede that love was beyond the realm of science. Not so, according to Dr. Lucy Brown, a professor in the department of neurology and neuroscience at the Albert Einstein College of Medicine in New York. She and her colleagues studied Magnetic Resonance Imaging (MRI) of lovers' brains and concluded that romantic love isn't so much an emotion as it is a drive based deep within our brains, right alongside our urges to find food and water.

"This helps explain why we do crazy things for love," Dr. Brown told Elizabeth Cohen, CNN Medical Correspondent. "Why did Edward VIII give up the throne for (American divorcee) Wallis Simpson? The systems that are built into us to find food and water are the things that were also active when he renounced the throne of England."

College students who professed to be in love underwent MRI scans while looking at a photo of their beloved. The scientists found that the caudate area of the brain – which is involved in cravings – became very active. Another area that lit up was the ventral tegmental, which produces dopamine, a powerful neuro-transmitter that affects pleasure and motivation. Dr. Brown told CNN that scientists believe that when you fall in love, the ventral tegmental floods the caudate with dopamine. The caudate then sends signals for more dopamine.

"The more dopamine you get, the more of a high you feel," Dr. Brown said. Or, as Dr. Helen Fisher put it: When you fall in love, "exactly the same system becomes active as when you take cocaine. You can feel intense elation when you're in love. You can feel intense elation when you're high on cocaine."

It seems love is just a chemical reaction in your brain, and a short-term one at that.

The author of "Anatomy of Love," Fisher describes love as nothing more than a brain-chemical cocktail of dopamine, norepi-nephrine and especially phenylethylamine (PEA).

Anthony Walsh, author of "The Science of Love: Understanding Love and Its Effects on Mind and Body," told Time Magazine that "PEA gives you that silly smile that you flash at strangers. When we meet someone who is attractive to us, the whistle blows at the PEA factory."

But phenylethylamine highs don't last forever, a fact that Time says lends support to arguments that passionate, romantic love is temporary. As with any amphetamine, the body builds up a tolerance to PEA. Soon, it takes more and more of the substance to produce love's special kick. After two to three years, the body simply can't crank up the needed amount of PEA. The bloom always falls off the rose. Fizzling chemicals spell the end of delirious passion. For many people, that marks the end of the liaison as well.

It's particularly true for those whom Dr. Michael Liebowitz of the New York State Psychiatric Institute terms "attraction junkies." They crave the intoxication of falling in love so much that they move frantically from one affair to the next, just as soon as the first rush of infatuation fades.

A similar vicious circle awaits you if you can't manage to find your way out of the thick forest that is Wanting, Receiving and Giving. The love you experience when you have combined all these steps is an illusion. The feelings of romantic love, as we've seen, are just chemicals triggered by a biological imperative to preserve the species.

You often believe you have all the answers when you're in love – whether it's passionate, sexual love or the kind of loved known as agape, a Greek word that means an unconditional love for everything. Your love consumes you, feels right, gives you a sense of completion, and makes the world beautiful. That's seductive, and like any addictive agent, it keeps you stuck in one place.

Without the benefit of any scientific data, we would guess from simple observation that at least 90 percent of the people in the world today are captured in the triangle of these three material steps and will never escape; it's an endless cycle of Wanting, Receiving and Giving.

They get up in the morning, trudge off to work so they can provide for their needs, allow themselves the occasional pleasure of vacations and material goods, raise their children the best they can, and lament that the spark has gone from their marriage. They want, receive and give, never understanding why they still feel this void in their soul. Deep inside, something's missing, but they don't know what it is. They look for comfort in religion, alcohol, drugs, sex or other escapist pursuits like television, movies and books. They run marathons, climb mountains, collect stamps, join knitting clubs, volunteer to help the needy, *anything* that will stop those incessant questions nagging the inner recesses of their mind.

All the time, the questions tug at them. Is this all there is? Why am I here? What's the meaning of life? Why do I feel like this isn't enough?

Chapter Thirteen

BALANCE

The best and safest thing is to keep a balance in your life, acknowledge the great powers around us and in us. If you can do that, and live that way, you are really a wise man.
Euripides

The big questions lead you to the edge of the universe. One minute you're cycling through the common stages of Wanting, Receiving and Giving, and the next, you're floating free. You have crossed the boundary and entered the spiritual world. Material concerns become unimportant. You understand without thinking, know without learning. You have escaped the trap, freed yourself from that world of illusion known as Maya. The material world shows itself to be transitory, an artificial construct whose substance is like a flimsy movie set. Behind the glitzy façade, there's nothing permanent, nothing of real substance.

This wisdom brings you into balance with your universe. The first seeds of true happiness begin to sprout – not the short-lived kind of happiness that comes from a pay raise or a new boyfriend or delicious meal, but a deep, lasting inner happiness born of understanding what really matters. To achieve this kind of balance, you must do two things:

1.   Recognize and accept that Wanting, Receiving and Giving will never lead to lasting fulfillment and satisfaction;
2.   Develop a mental approach that allows you to transcend the world of linear thinking. You have to learn how to silence your outward senses and merge with the frequency of the Absolute.

Even if you still harbor some doubts about all of this, you probably can sense the logic of No. 1. Most people will recognize its truth in the deep recesses of their mind and soul, where they hide their uneasiness. They know they're not blissfully happy, they know that greed can lead to insatiable desire, and they know that material goods aren't the answer.

So let's move on to No. 2, where the key to freedom lies. The mental approach that allows you to transcend all the mundane silliness of the human condition can come in many forms: meditation, hypnosis, spiritual ecstasy, prayer, mind-control techniques, sensory deprivation, yoga, channeling, out-of-body experiences, or even psychoactive drugs or plants.

I do not recommend the method I used – drinking tea made with cobra venom – and we certainly don't advocate the use of opiates, LSD, peyote, mescaline or other illegal substances, because there are much healthier and safer techniques for silencing the endless chatter of one's senses.

Undoubtedly, you have already experienced altered states of consciousness without even giving it much thought. There's nothing spooky or necessarily "New Age" about it. An altered state can be triggered by indigestion, fever, sleep deprivation, starvation, oxygen deprivation, nitrogen narcosis (from deep-water diving), or a traumatic accident.

Or it can occur naturally, in a much more mundane way. If you've ever been driving a car and suddenly realized that your mind was so lost in thought that you don't remember the last several miles or making any turns, you have experienced an altered state of consciousness. It's a form of self-hypnosis wherein your subconscious takes over the task of driving while your conscious mind goes somewhere else. So there's no question you can do this. Everybody can, as long as they're not brain-damaged.

Later in this chapter, we're going to offer a couple of meditation techniques you can try. These are just suggestions. We recommend you explore the subject much more deeply on your own and experiment with other methods. The goal is to gain an inner knowledge that a higher reality exists beyond the realm of your senses, and that you can go there. It doesn't really matter which path you take. When your mind touches this higher reality for the first time, even if it's for just a brief moment, you finally understand what we mean when we refer to an experience that's beyond words.

Actually, you probably already know this experience, too; you go there for a few fleeting moments during an orgasm. It's called a "climax," appropriately enough, because it's the highest mental, emotional and physical experience most people ever know. Every cell in your body becomes focused in a single direction – true, undistracted bliss.

Some religious visionaries seem to experience a similar kind of transcendent state when they enter the frenzy or "delirium" of spiritual ecstasy. Author Deng Ming-Dao ("Gateway to a Vast World") sees these fleeting moments of bliss as stepping-stones, not the final goal.

"Eroticism and spirituality – the two deepest endeavors of humanity – are twins," Ming-Dao wrote. "Both eroticism and spirituality mean intense involvement in the diversity and color of the world. But there is a higher order, a state where one is holiness itself. Then nothing of the world of color matters to you anymore. The pleasures of the couch will mean nothing. Neither will the glories of the ascetic's efforts mean anything. Only by entering the colorless state of pure, blinding light can there be freedom from the twins.

"Meditation changes your consciousness. The type of consciousness that emerges depends on the meditation. Your consciousness in turn colors your perceptions of the world around you. There is no such thing as objective reality. You color everything. If you want the highest state of being, aim for consciousness without color."

Ming-Dao doesn't see "colorless" as a bland or boring vision, but more as the white light of pure wisdom and inner peace.

As you become balanced, you exist in a state where you don't want anything, and nothing troubles you. You're in a space with no pressure. That's the very definition of balance – equilibrium. You're like a planet orbiting its sun ... a perfect sphere, spinning on its axis. Up is down, down is up, everything is in synch, and you're perfectly satisfied.

Stuck on Earth and confined by gravity, we experience this illusion that there really exists an "up" and "down." In the weightlessness of space, those terms cease to have meaning. That's what it feels like to be balanced. Up, down, left, right, good, bad ... all these words become just limited degrees of perception. Their meanings are arbitrary and artificial.

"Balance" can be a confusing stage. People get there and think, "Wow, I don't stick to the world anymore. It's different. I wanted to have all that power, and now I have it, but it doesn't mean anything." If you accept it and don't sell yourself out, you can pass this stage and move ever closer to Oneness. You can go to the place of not Wanting anymore and enjoy the pleasure of living without artificial need.

But just as there was temptation in the step of Giving and love, there are dangers when you taste Balance for the first time. Recall the examples of Rajneesh, the guru from Pune, and the Maharishi Mahesh Yogi, who tutored The Beatles and other celebrities. Both elevated their souls to a level seldom seen, but as their power expanded exponentially, they seemed to lose their balance. Rajneesh indulged his taste for luxuries and Rolls-Royces, and the Maharishi allegedly made sexual advances on actress Mia Farrow and other women who came to him for spiritual guidance.

Author Paul Saltzman ("The Beatles in Rishikesh"), who met with The Beatles and others at the Maharishi's India retreat, wrote: "To the Beatles, the Maharishi's apparent sexuality was the heavy straw that broke the camel's back. They had earlier been concerned about two things: the Maharishi using them to promote himself, and what seemed to be his focus on money, unexpected by them in a spiritual teacher or holy man."

The lesson to be learned is this: Achieving Balance and maintaining Balance are two completely different things. The first is relatively easy, the second enormously challenging. The world's material and earthly pleasures will try to push and pull at you constantly. Reaching the state of Balance is your first step into the spiritual world, but you're still not completely disconnected from the material world.

First, you were like a car that needs gas (motivation from the material world) to go anywhere. Then you found Balance and became a car that could go anywhere you wanted – without gas. You found that a truly fulfilled existence is effortless, as long as you remain in Balance.

To take this step into the spiritual world, we need the help of a tool that can silence our senses. Meditation is perhaps the safest and healthiest such tool. Thousands of different meditative techniques can be found by the persistent seeker. Experiment on your own until you find the method that's most effective for you.

Here are some examples:

Step-By-Step Instructions for Meditation Technique from Intelegen, Inc., a Michigan company which markets audio recordings designed to induce altered states of consciousness.

1. The sitting posture which has been found most effective for attaining tranquility quickly is the half-lotus. This position (with some practice) allows you to sit still for a long time without aches or pain. Rest your right leg on the left one, with your back erect. Your hands should rest palms-upward on your lap. The tip of your right index finger should be in gentle contact with the tip of your left thumb. This hand position serves as an alarm: if you should suddenly get drowsy, finger and thumb will push together, warning you to avoid falling into a mindless slumber. If the half-lotus position is really too uncomfortable for you, it is better to choose another more comfortable position. The important thing is to make sure, whatever position you adopt, that your back is straight and your body is relaxed without feeling sleepy.

2. Keep your consciousness steady, and softly close your eyes. Relax every part of your body, beginning with the muscles of your face. Then relax the muscles of your neck, your shoulders, and your arms, right down to the tips of your fingers. Relax your chest, your abdomen and your legs, right down to the tips of your toes. Make sure all parts of your body

are relaxed.

3. Feel as if you are sitting alone in the world, and the air around your body is made up of tiny particles of happiness and joy. Slowly inhale into your body a full and gentle breath. As you breath in, feel that you are breathing in those tiny particles of happiness and joy. Feel that inside your body, there is just an empty space, with no muscles, no organs, no tissues. Feel that the breath is filling your body with happiness and joy. As you breath out, feel that the out-breath is carrying away all troubles, all worries, all thoughts. Inside your body is just an empty space filled with happiness and joy. Relax your mind from every thought, and continue to maintain this state for as long as you can. With your eyes closed, you will find that your mind travels from one idea to another, and when it wanders, the ideas upon which the mind dwells will influence the feelings, the emotions and the state of happiness in the mind. Meditation is the means we use to take control of our mind to stop our thoughts from wandering. The basis of all methods of meditation is to concentrate the mind upon a single object or a single idea, and it is the inherent qualities of this object or idea that will lead you to success in meditation. We will use a crystal ball as an object of meditation because it has the inherent qualities of brightness and clarity, and will encourage the mind to be bright and clear, too. Simultaneously, to keep the mind flowing toward a state of happiness and calm, we repeat in our mind the word "Samma-Araham," which means the "righteous Absolute of Attainment that a human being can achieve."

4. Open your eyes slowly. Look carefully at a crystal ball (a real one, if you have it, or one you visualize in your imagination). Notice the shape, the purity, the clarity and the brightness of the crystal ball as if you are taking a photograph of it in the deepest part of your mind. Then close your eyes again and relax.

5. Slowly visualize the crystal ball floating in front of your face. Mentally, reduce the size of the crystal ball until its size is smaller than the tip of your little finger. Imagine that the crystal

ball is floating in front of your nostril – the right nostril for men and the left one for women.

6. Visualize that the crystal ball moves inside your nostril. It moves along inside your nostril, and when it reaches the bridge of your nose, it stops still, suspended in silence. Make your crystal ball as bright and clear as you can. Listen to the sound of "Samma-Araham" as you repeat it three times in your mind.

7. Now, slowly move the crystal ball backward until it arrives at the point in the very center of your head. Here, the crystal ball stops still, suspended in silence. Make the crystal ball as bright and clear as you can. Listen to the sound of "Samma-Araham" as you repeat it three times in your mind.

8. Now slowly, visualize the crystal ball as it floats downward until it reaches the back part of the roof of your mouth. Here, the crystal ball pauses. Make the crystal ball as bright and clear as you can. Listen to the sound of "Samma-Araham" three times, a soothing sound that seems to come from the very center of your body.

9. Now, slowly move the crystal ball farther downward until it reaches the central part of your throat. Again, the crystal ball pauses in silence. Make the crystal ball as bright and as clear as you can. Again, listen to the sound of "Samma-Araham" three times.

10. Now, slowly move the crystal ball deep down into your body. It floats slowly and gently downward, like a bubble, deeper into your throat, deeper into your chest, deeper into your body. In the central part of your body, you imagine two lines. The first one runs from your navel directly out through your lower back. The second line runs from your right side to your left, and the two lines intersect at a point no larger than the eye of a needle. Your crystal ball moves downward until the point of intersection is at the center of the crystal ball. Make the crystal ball as bright and as clear as you can. Again, you listen to the sound of "Samma-Araham" three times.

11. Move the crystal ball upward a distance equal to two finger breadths, to a point you see as the very center of your

body. You will not move the crystal ball anywhere else. Allow it to remain here in calm and peace. Constantly observe the clarity, purity and brightness of the crystal ball. Always make the crystal ball as bright and clear as you can. Listen to the sound of "Samma-Araham" over and over again, as if the sound is coming from deep in the center of the crystal ball. The crystal ball will become brighter and brighter, clearer and clearer, until it is as if you see it with your own eyes. At this stage, you will soon find the crystal ball sparkling and shining like a diamond. This stage is called the Initial Path. At this stage, the mind is firmly established on the shining crystal ball, which in turn is firmly seated at the center of the body. You will touch upon happiness. After continuously paying attention at the center of the crystal ball, see it slowly peel away a succession of layers, each more pure than the last, until it reaches the Ultimate One, the highest level of supreme happiness forever and ever, which is now within you.

Breathe deeply, and slowly bring your awareness back to your arms, legs, body and your surroundings. Move slowly as you rejoin the world, still carrying the purity of the Ultimate One within you.

Here is a different approach, for those who are more comfortable with a process that doesn't rely so much on visualization:

"How to Meditate," by James Quirk, author of "How to Breathe Like a Yoga Master."

Meditating a few minutes each day is a proven stress reducer, and it can improve your outlook on life as well. There are as many different meditation methods as there are instructors, but if all you need is a basic, universal method, here's an easy way to get started.

1. Create a quiet, relaxing environment. Turn off any TV sets or other noisy appliances. Some soft, relaxing music is OK, but it isn't necessary. Make sure your cell phone is off.

2. Sit on a chair or a cushion. You don't have to twist your limbs into the lotus position or adopt any unusual postures (but

you can if it's comfortable).

3. Close your eyes or find something else calm to look at. You may want to use a small candle flame.

4. Take care to sit erect, allowing for free and easy breathing. This will happen naturally when your knees are below the level of your waist. Don't try lying down; most people will fall asleep meditating in this position.

5. Observe your breath. Don't try to change the way you are breathing, just let your attention rest on the flow of your breath. The goal is to allow the "chattering" in your mind to gradually fade away.

6. Relax every muscle in your body. Don't rush this, as it takes time to fully relax, and relax bit by bit, starting at your toes, and working up to your head.

7. Mentally focus on words that appeal to your linguistic style. If you are visual, use words that evoke pictures. If you are auditory, use words that evoke sound. If you are kinesthetic, use words that evoke feelings.

8. Repeat these words to yourself to encourage the outcome that you desire. For example, repeat to yourself how relaxed you are by saying, "I am completely relaxed."

9. Visualize a place that calms you. It can be real or imaginary. This step can replace word-repetition, augment it or be excluded from your meditation. One option is to imagine you are at the top of a staircase leading down to a peaceful place of bliss and contentment. Count your way down the steps until you are relaxed and at peace.

Tips

Ideally, you want to achieve a state free from distracting thoughts, but this takes a lot of practice. When a thought pops into your mind, don't try to block it or force it out. Just observe it impartially and let it go away of its own accord. If you don't become attached to your thoughts, they will fade away without creating more thoughts.

You can meditate anytime you have a few spare moments.

Try it at work for a quick stress reducer.

For most people, closing the eyes is best, but some prefer to observe a candle flame or a similar relaxing sight. You can also allow your eyes to rest where they naturally fall with your head held at a comfortable angle.

When meditating, try to stop thinking, in the same the way you stop talking. In your head, just stop saying anything to yourself. It might be harder than it sounds, but it gets easier with practice. There's a lot of truth in silence. You can go for awareness walks every day, where you just try to be as aware of your surroundings as possible with all five senses. This also helps ground and quiet the mind and stop the internal chatter.

Meditation = Total Relaxation + Total Alertness.

Children can usually meditate extremely easily, but only when they understand what to do.

Once you learn to meditate well enough, you can slip into a state of meditation in seconds, which is very helpful.

Take a meditation retreat of at least a few days. Some of these are silent, others are not. Once you experience the feeling of meditation, you will better know how and if it applies to your life.

Meditation may be useful if you have trouble falling asleep. While lying in bed, follow the steps for a meditation, and remove any anxiety about falling asleep. Before you know it, it'll be morning!

Warnings

Don't try to meditate for hours on end when you first begin, as this can lead to burnout. A few minutes each day is enough to get you started.

Don't expect immediate results. The purpose of meditation is not to turn you into a Zen master overnight. Meditation works best when it is done for its own sake, without becoming attached to results.

Avoid groups with cult-like practices or that are involved with other psychic activities like spirit channeling or mediums.

Meditation opens up your mind and body to psychic influences, and some groups might use this to initiate you into relationships with their leaders and spirit guides without making this clear.

Things You'll Need

A room without distractions.

A comfortable spot to sit.

A candle, picture or photograph (optional)

We mentioned in the Preface that this is not a Get-Spiritually-Rich-Quick book. The first three steps to wisdom and inner peace can be understood and conquered simply by education, understanding and perhaps opening your mind to new and strange ideas. But the middle step, Balance, likely will take longer. Becoming adept at achieving an altered state of consciousness takes practice. Being able to slide into deep meditation at a moment's notice usually requires a trained and focused mind.

Yet this is not always the case. Some people have a natural talent for it, or perhaps an inborn understanding. Some neophytes take to meditation instantly and can become masters almost overnight. Your results may vary.

The goals of your meditation practice are to:

1. Turn off the faucet of thoughts that continually flood your brain.
2. Learn how to operate that faucet at will, so you can reach your place of peaceful quietude on command.
3. Learn how to shut down your sensory inputs one by one – sight, sound, touch, smell, taste.
4. Be able to combine your peaceful stillness and your silenced senses, so that you exist in a state without any outside or inside stimuli.

Once you are able to reach this state of complete "letting go," something magical will happen: Without any effort, you will transcend the material world and feel at one with this Absolute presence that mystics have been speaking about for more than 2,500 years.

The beauty of this out-of-body experience is that it just occurs naturally, all by itself. There's nothing you can do to make it happen, except to stop "trying." We guarantee it will happen to you the instant you are able to silence your mind and senses completely.

As you refine these techniques, at some point a realization will dawn upon you: Your inner spirit, your true self, has reached a state of blissful Balance. The Wanting, Receiving and Giving that dominated your life previously are no longer meaningful. They may still exist, but they are irrelevant. Real happiness floods into every cell in your body because you know you have found Balance.

The realization that you have indeed moved into the spiritual step of Balance will come from a combination of knowledge, understanding, acceptance and, most important of all, your spiritual connection to the Absolute.

You will not remain balanced every minute of every day. Initially, you may only feel balance during meditation and perhaps for several minutes or hours afterward. But with practice, the peaceful balance will stay with you longer and longer, until it becomes a major part of your life.

Continue reading through the following steps and chapters of this book while you experiment with types of meditation. Absorb the concepts and continue to apply them to your own universe.

Chapter Fourteen

SATISFACTION

Whatever satisfies the soul is truth.
Walt Whitman

Sometimes we call this the step of "So What?" You have examined, understood and transcended the steps of Wanting, Receiving and Giving, and as your command of an effective meditation technique grows, you find yourself spending more and more time in the blissful state of Balance. And then you start to look at the world of temptation around you and say, "So what?"

This indicates you are effortlessly moving forward into the step of Satisfaction. The world looks vastly different. It's as if you spent your whole life wearing colored glasses, and now you've removed them and for the first time see things as they really are. What matters to most people no longer matters to you.

When you reach Satisfaction, your world gets bigger. You might see a physically gorgeous person, and while everyone else gathers around that person, you instinctively realize that beauty is irrelevant when it comes to the only real, organic goal of everyone and everything: achieving Balance. In fact, beauty is less than irrelevant; it actually can be a hindrance, because physical beauty will easily distract a person from Balance.

Wealth, praise, accomplishment and other egocentric achievements also can pull a person out of Balance just as readily as desires and addictions. Satisfaction is knowing that enough is enough. You don't need the whole cosmos. You know you can keep your own little universe in balance, so you do that. At this level, we each have our own universe.

The Sufi mystic and poet Jalal ad-Din Rumi said, "It may be that the satisfaction I need depends on my going away, so that when I've gone and come back, I'll find it at home."

It's almost as simple as Dorothy in "The Wizard of Oz"

journeying through all kinds of adventures to reach the Great and Powerful Wizard, only to find that real satisfaction lies in understanding that there's no place like home. But it's not *quite* that simple.

Until now, satisfaction probably meant a smug feeling that followed some concrete occurrence, like closing a deal at work, buying your first house, or watching your team win the World Cup. But in the hierarchy of the 7 Steps to Wisdom and Inner Peace, Satisfaction is more like an absence of feelings you formerly had. It's addition by subtraction.

Once you take away Wanting, Receiving, and Giving as motivating forces in your life, you're no longer pulled in so many useless directions. The frenzy departs from your brain, leaving you with a void to fill, and Satisfaction is what flows in to fill it. This will be the easiest step yet for you to experience and then transcend.

The first three steps of the material word are so deeply ingrained in our psyche that releasing them requires a lot of thought and meditation. Your mind has to leap to a level you probably have never experienced before. But once you've finally acquired the experience of Balance, you'll have broken free from the chains that tied you to the Earth.

Sliding from Balance into Satisfaction will occur naturally, and probably very quickly. One day you'll see something that used to trigger the "desire" response inside your brain and realize with a smile that you've become immune to it. Instead of lusting after the beautiful person who walks by, you'll think, "So what?"

If you're not quite there yet, that last sentence might actually make you laugh. Are we saying that sexual drives become non-existent once we've reached the final three steps? How can one have true happiness without the pleasures of the body?

The secret is that true happiness is much deeper and permanent than pleasures of the body. When you are truly living in the step of Satisfaction, it's like having that blissful post-orgasm feeling all the time. You're body is relaxed, your mind is at ease, and primal urges no longer gnaw at your insides. Yes, you will still enjoy sexual union, but the fact of the matter is, you'll enjoy everything.

The sensation of taking a bite of humble bread crust will feel like an orgasm. You'll welcome the sustenance into your body with slow, purposeful chewing. Your taste buds will explode in pleasure as your salivary glands begin to melt the bread into your mouth. With eyes closed, you can almost feel the nutrients giving new life to your cells. When that first bite is well-chewed and gently swallowed, you have another orgasm. The bread and you are one. It's a sacred experience.

Contrast this to the way most of us eat – shoveling down our gullets large forkfuls of processed foods we neither look at nor think about. As we consume these empty calories, we're watching TV or reading or talking. The food itself is barely an afterthought.

And we wonder why Americans are plagued by indigestion and obesity?

At the level of Satisfaction, you see the miraculous in the mundane. Everything contributes to your happiness. The flight of a hummingbird, the sound of the rain, the breath of wind through a tree – all these things feed your sense of satisfaction.

Sexual pleasure – yes, of course, this also provides you with heightened satisfaction, but it's not necessarily better than the sound of children's laughter in the park – just different. Once you've reached the level of Satisfaction as it's known in Step 5, everything satisfies you.

Everything? Yes, everything. Even the so-called tragedies of life can be recognized as part of the inevitable and natural flow of the universe, and your satisfaction in experiencing them comes from knowing a higher reality connects everything, and that neither you nor anything else in the universe is separate from this reality. If you have truly reached Satisfaction, you'll accept even the untimely death of a loved one as natural, irreversible and, in its own way, satisfying. If you understand that we're all part of the same universal Force and that matter can be neither created nor destroyed, you'll accept that nothing vanishes – it just changes.

We realize the concept of that previous paragraph will seem completely out of step with the masses. Humans grieve death because they feel "a part of them" has died, too. This is the ego talking. We are in the process of leaving ego behind, because true freedom is impossible as long as you have an ego that's saying, "it's all about me."

You are nothing. At the same time, you are everything. The Force flows on within you and without you. When you become one with the Absolute, there is nothing greater than yourself, but at the same time, there is nothing more insignificant. Your greatness comes from the panoply of existence that flows in your veins and animates your cells. It's as if you were a tiny stitch in the grand quilt of the universe. If you identify yourself as a single stitch, you're so insignificant that you could disappear tomorrow and the universe would not even notice. But if you identify yourself as the quilt – not part of the quilt, but the quilt itself – you are God.

This is the realization that manifests itself as pure Satisfaction. Everything that occurs in the life of the puny stitch can be greeted with a non-judgmental, "So what?" Not even incidents that before would have seemed cataclysmic, like floods or earthquakes, can destroy you.

Your "So what?" doesn't dismiss death and disaster as boring. Indeed, the fabric of human existence remains endlessly fascinating, and you care for your fellow man as much as ever – perhaps more so, because you realize you're truly all One – but you don't anguish over the tragic acts of "an unjust God" because you understand and accept the flow of the Force.

We compare it to the experience of a surfer riding a wave. He never tries to fight the power of the wave and drive it backward. It would grind him flat into the sand every time. But once he understands how to harness the flow and power of the water, he can perform tricks and stunts and feel the exhilaration of speed. Some things you can control, others you cannot. Like a surfer, you can take the Force for the ride of your life, but only if you accept the direction of the waves. Don't cry because the swell is breaking from the south. Ride the wave that you're given, and do it with joy.

Not fully at this level yet? No worries. Effort is not required. If you continue to nurture the feeling of Balance from your meditation practice, Satisfaction will arise spontaneously. It's a natural progression as you move ever-closer to Oneness.

Each of the final three steps feeds your soul directly into the next one. During your progression through the first three steps, it's like you're climbing toward the top of a water slide. You reach the top as you find Balance; you're no longer driven by the urge to climb. Then the rest of the trip is like gliding down the water slide. You might not even be able to stop yourself as you cascade toward Oneness.

Ponder, for a moment, this concept of everything in the universe being connected and, in effect, one single organism. This is one of the most important keys to Satisfaction. By visualizing and accepting this, you realize there's no need to want anything, because you already have everything. You don't keep it in a bag at your home, but everything in the universe is your birthright. It's part of you.

You have everything, and you have nothing, because you don't need or covet. Some of these ideas may need to sink in over time, but the main reason we felt we could share them with you in book form is that we believe they're all supported by logic. You might have to experience that connection to the Absolute to understand it, but belief and emotion can only take you so far. At some point, it has to make perfect sense.

In Rhonda Byrne's best-selling book and movie DVD, "The Secret," she suggests that you can get anything you want by "the Law of Attraction," which is a new spin on Norman Vincent Peale's old "Power of Positive Thinking." The gist of it seems to be: If you really, *really* want a new Lamborghini, it will come into your life. Just focus on it. This concept is incomplete, at best.

While we appreciate "The Secret" as far as it goes, the kind of sea-change in your life that we're pursuing here won't happen just because you wish for it. You have to walk the path step by step.

We also see value in the work of motivational speakers like Anthony Robbins and writers like Deepak Chopra, but how many people experience their work, feel inspired for a little while, and then go back to their same old routines? We're not interested in getting you emotionally excited about the idea of attaining Oneness with the universe, only to forget about it a week or two after you've finished the book.

These 7 Steps promise wisdom and inner peace. The only proof of that will be your own true experience. We want you to know the feeling of Balance then slide beyond that into Satisfaction. This is the beginning of inner peace and happiness – real, lasting happiness that can't be shaken by outside circumstances.

Continue practicing your meditation techniques, recognize the signs of Balance as they come into your life, and revel in the inner peace that Satisfaction brings. You may linger here for as long as you wish, but inevitably, you will reach a point when you start to feel Detachment.

Chapter Fifteen

DETACHMENT

He who would be serene and pure needs but one thing, detachment.
Meister Eckhart

Let's check your inner-peace pulse. You've already experimented with different meditation techniques and settled on one that works best. You've succeeded at least once in shutting down all your sensory inputs. At that moment, a new sensation took over your being: you returned to your source and temporarily lost your individuality. You finally understood, if only for a moment, what it means to become one with the Absolute.

This usually is such a transcendent event that your consciousness is never again quite the same. It sets you on a course that leads you deeper and deeper into your inner universe, which you come to realize is the same as the entire outer universe. You are a star-child, a universal consciousness, matter and void, God and nothingness.

If you haven't quite kissed this kind of sky yet, feel free to read on, or go back, or continue to explore various meditation techniques and depths. The path is yours, and the choice is yours. We want you to check your inner-peace pulse at this point so you may see how you're doing, but no matter where you're at, you may continue to explore the chapters on these final two spiritual-world steps and the chapters that follow.

Our hope is that you will keep using this book as a reference tool. Move backward and forward at will. Review sections that didn't fully sink in. Go at your own pace. Nothing is required except whatever you wish to give.

Traversing the 7 Steps should not seem challenging. It should seem like pure joy. As you continue to progress, you probably will feel a proverbial wind beneath your wings, blowing you effortlessly toward the wisdom and inner peace you seek.

Eventually, you will feel detached from the process itself. This is the beginning of Step 6. At one point, you were feeling as if you were making a conscious effort to follow the steps, and then one day, you suddenly realized you have completely let go. You're no longer attached to the goal, the process, or anything else.

This Detachment is a more advanced form of the freedom you began to experience in Balance and Satisfaction – much more profound, and definitely different. It seems to follow naturally after one moves through the level of Satisfaction. This is where you find a state of equilibrium and peace that's no longer based on Satisfaction. The very name of the previous step couldn't exist without its opposite, dissatisfaction.

Satisfaction implies a complacency based on your newfound lack of perceived need. At the level of Satisfaction, you could walk around in the real world, constantly bathed in serenity, and still not seem drastically different from the people around you. But once you reach Detachment, you feel like you've parted company with your fellow men and women. You walk alone. Everyone around you remains invested in the fabric of life, but you no longer see any of it as significant.

Before, perhaps your friends merely thought you and your mind-control games were just a little goofy. Now they're convinced you're swimming against the flow. And they're right.

The rest of human civilization swims with the flow chosen by its given social context. We could use the hackneyed comparison of a herd of cattle or lemmings following their leaders in a charge over a cliff, but it's true that most people embrace the customs and belief systems in which they are enmeshed. Even the occasional self-righteous iconoclast or social boat-rocker will only take his civil disobedience so far.

People are afraid to follow the white rabbit so far down the hole that they fall head-first into Wonderland. They're afraid of being so different that almost no one can relate to them.

Can you imagine someone so completely detached from the

norm that he believes there's nothing in the material world that really matters? Can you imagine someone who believes that we can all progress into a higher form of consciousness so evolved that our bodies become superfluous? Someone who believes that one day, we can all vibrate on the same wavelength and know intuitively that aggression and war, for any cause, would be unthinkable?

This kind of person would be an outcast of the highest order. She would be dismissed as a fool, or perhaps insane. This would be a person who has left her reason and logic behind. This would be you ... if you choose to continue following us down the rabbit hole.

Detachment plucks you out of the flow of your civilization, because you no longer see the world in the same terms as the masses. You no longer see humans as imperfect beings aspiring to follow some image of a perfect God, or some manmade system of laws. In fact, you no longer see human beings as separate entities at all.

We are all just part of the Flow, and we're moving in a direction that was rendered inevitable by everything that came before. There's no sense in criticizing the human race for its murderous and self-destructive ways. We're just part of the universal energy source that is trying to balance itself. The imbalance isn't a problem, just a fact. Our tendency to move toward greater balance isn't altruistic, just a fact. We are doing what all energy has always done – react to imbalances by shifting toward the direction of balance.

We believe that all the spiritual leaders over the last 10,000 years who preached peace, transcendental states of consciousness and the attainment of Oneness were just expressions of the human force trying to balance itself. The urge to move toward balance continues today with our pursuits, and yours, right here and now. The seeker who begins to realize this eventually may enter a realm of Detachment.

Imagine a patient in a hospital, hooked up to monitors that read his life signs. When the heart is beating and the brain is functioning, the monitors show peaks and valleys. It's like the journey of life itself – all peaks and valleys. Disconnect all those monitors, and they show flat lines. That's like your psyche after Detachment. Universal truth is like the background radiation of the Big Bang: a constant, steady, peaceful hum.

When you reach Detachment, the deep valleys of your sadness and depression disappear. The high peaks of elation and excitement also disappear. True wisdom and inner peace feels like a contented, unshakeable, flat-line smile all the time.

Humanists love to tell stories of the tumbling emotions that make a person truly human – the tears of heartbreak, the joy of love, the flash of anger and stab of fear. Their poems and novels and films provide a rich tapestry that celebrates the human condition. To deny all this is to enter Detachment. This is where you part company with the mainstream.

We believe that all those human peak-and-valley emotions that we experience are just necessary baby steps in the evolution of our consciousness. The baby steps are meaningful, but at some point they will be left behind.

Those peak-and-valley emotions trigger the wars, murders and destruction that have kept us out of balance for eons. How much safer would our corporeal existence become if we eliminated the fear of others, the love of nationalism, the zeal of religious fanaticism, and insatiable greed? If the entire planetary population became detached, the next step inevitably would be Oneness.

In evaluating the duality of emotion and logic in the human mind, we are reminded of themes expressed by the characters in the "Star Trek" movies and television series. In "The Return of Physics to the Tao," author Jim Beichler wrote:

> "Spock, Doctor McCoy and Captain Kirk, the three main characters of the (Star Trek) stories, were actually three aspects of a single entity or mind. Spock was logic, pure reason trying to subdue emotion, but at his core, a small amount of emotion could always be discerned. Doc McCoy was motivated

primarily by emotion, but he was also a scientist deep down inside, at his own center. As the characters faced different problems, Spock sometimes saved the day through logic, and the other times McCoy's emotionalism was central to the plot.

"But Captain Kirk, who mediated between emotion and logic (or science), was the true hero. Kirk was the physical manifestation of a synthesis of the two opposites, so he ultimately resolved all the problems, sometimes leaning more toward logic (and Spock), and sometimes leaning more toward emotion (and McCoy's point of view). Such a dynamic interplay of opposites is one of the underlying principles of all the great literature from Homer's "Odysseus" to Roddenberry's "Star Trek" and beyond, a fact which clearly demonstrates the universality and the dynamism of opposites as far as humans are concerned. Very seldom does any problem in our own world find its solution in pure logic or pure emotion, but a combination of the two."

At the level of Detachment, we find an equilibrium between the logic of Spock and the emotion of McCoy. Kirk prevails.

While the concepts of our 7 Steps to Wisdom and Inner Peace may appear to be wispy and New-Age at times, we categorize them firmly in the realm of reason. We have examined and dissected them with logic, and we subjected them to scrutiny by science, philosophy and theology (See Chapter 19).

In the end, we share the conclusion that Beichler reached after reading more than half a dozen studies on the science of physics as it compares with and contrasts to mysticism. Beichler wrote:

"Modern physics and mysticism are approaching the same view of reality ... It has taken science more than two millennia of investigation to come to the same conclusions as the mystics. The mystics accept the fact that consciousness underlies physical reality and therefore assume that the opposites we find in nature are illusory. So they intuitively transcend the opposites to experience that consciousness and understand reality.

"Many scientists have long suspected that there is more to physical reality than the mechanisms described in physics. Yet only in the past century has that realization been forced upon the whole of physics through the development of relativity theory and quantum mechanics. It now seems evident to physicists that consciousness is at least intimately related to physical reality, if not actually the basis of reality. So mysticism and physics now show many similarities of worldview."

Consider that phrase at the end of the penultimate sentence of the previous paragraph: "...consciousness is at least intimately related to physical reality, if not *actually the basis of reality*." This goes to the heart of our point. Consciousness is the basis of reality; therefore, you can control your reality by controlling your consciousness.

Controlling our own reality is exactly what we have been doing as we transcend each stop along our path of the 7 Steps. Reality alters according to the changes in our consciousness.

When you were consumed by Wanting, Receiving and Giving, you and your world were defined by those activities. When you finally achieved Balance, the world started to transform. All your pressures eased. That led to Satisfaction, in which you felt like you had finally found the key to happiness.

Now, as you move into Detachment, you realize happiness is a relative term based on your relationship, or lack of relationship, to events, people and material goods. Happiness – once perceived as the goal – now reveals itself as a mere stepping stone to wisdom and inner peace. There's a big difference.

When you detach from all material concerns, you feel like an impartial observer gazing at the Absolute with your first fully realized sense of understanding. You see, sense and comprehend that we're all just dancing expressions of the same energy force. You're just a patch of the universe that is aware of itself. You accept that the urge to achieve Balance is our only universal drive.

All this is viewed dispassionately. It's not good or bad to any degree; it simply is what it is. You are detached from it, a peaceful observer. But then something magical happens. What you observe guides you one step further. Detachment has allowed you to gaze into the eyes of the Absolute, and it calls you to meld with it. You are about to complete the circle that started before your birth. You are about to become one with the universe.

Chapter Sixteen

ONENESS

Those who see all creatures within themselves
And themselves in all creatures know no fear.
Those who see all creatures in themselves
And themselves in all creatures know no grief.
How can the multiplicity of life
Delude the one who sees its unity?
Isha Upanishad 6-7

When we came across the above passage from the Upanishads –
part of the Hindu scriptures – we realized just how ancient this
quest for Oneness truly is. Those words were written sometime
between 2,400 and 2,800 years ago.

While the quest has always been an individual and lonely one
that continues even today (as evidenced by you reading this text),
it is definitely attainable. Oneness has been achieved by countless
seekers. We believe Rumi, the Buddha, Jesus and Mohammad have
walked as one with the universe. Tens of thousands of others have
tasted this experience with lesser notoriety.

We realize our journey toward wisdom and inner peace is a
metaphysical "travel within" which may seem to part company
with logic and reason, so we want to digress for a moment to show
you that what appears to be pure mysticism is actually supported
by science.

You are a 21st Century person, so we have a 21st Century
example of Oneness that might make sense to those entrenched in
the digital Information Age. It's a concept called the Worldwide
Mind.

Some researchers believe that one day, it will be possible to link
every human mind in the world through wireless transmission.
Just as the Worldwide Web can connect every computer in the

world, the Worldwide Mind could connect every human brain in the world.

The distinction between individuals would blur. If my thoughts can become your thoughts and vice versa, our brains are joined. If everyone has direct access to the intelligence of everybody else on the planet, are we not one single organism?

Instead of using email, a friend could transmit his thoughts directly into your head. You could "download" information, ideas and even emotions from any other person, directly into your brain, at will. It's science fiction rapidly becoming science fact.

Are you familiar with those scenes in the popular film "The Matrix," when characters had a cable plugged directly into a port on the backs of their heads? They could access any kind of knowledge or skill-set that the mainframe computer provided. By just sitting quietly while his brain downloaded the information, actor Keanu Reeves' "Neo" character was able to open his eyes and say, "This is amazing. I know Kung Fu." When Neo and the Trinity character (actress Carrie-Ann Moss) needed a quick escape from the bad guys and only had access to a helicopter, Neo breathlessly asked, "Can you fly that thing?" "Not yet," she answered. She summoned the Operator by phone and said, "Tank, I need a pilot program for a military M-109 helicopter." Her eyes fluttered, and seconds later, she was flying the helicopter like an ace. This kind of technology is theoretically possible. Many of the obstacles that kept it in the realm of science fiction have been resolved.

Rodolfo Llinas, Professor of Neuroscience and Chairman of the department of Physiology & Neuroscience at the NYU School of Medicine, has developed bundles of nanowires thinner than spider webs that can be inserted into the blood vessels of human brains. These could transfer digital information that arrives at an implanted wireless receiver in your head. It would be true Random Access Memory.

Mapping of the human brain has enabled researchers to pinpoint the locations of many types of thought, cognition and sensory experience. Human brain function is electro-chemical, and we've already figured out how to electrically stimulate portions of the brain to trigger specific sights, sounds, scents and emotions. Reality is nothing more than what your brain tells you is real, and if an electrical stimulation of the "scent" part of your brain triggers the aroma of coffee, you smell coffee. The coffee isn't really there, but for you, the aroma is.

"Direct communication with the deep recesses of the brain may not be so far off," Dr. Llinas said. "What does this mean for the future? Deep brain stimulation could create the ultimate virtual reality."

Direct communication between man and machine is already happening. After suffering a major brain stem stroke in an auto accident, an Atlanta 16-year-old named Eric was paralyzed and unable to communicate in any way, although he was still aware of everything going on around him.

Surgeons implanted an electrode in his brain that interfaced with a computer via wireless connection. Just by thinking about what he wanted to say, Eric was able to send a signal to the computer, which used new software to translate his signals into words.

The next step would be connecting human brains directly to other human brains. The U.S. government is taking it so seriously that the National Security Agency sent agents to the lab at the Massachusetts Institute of Technology where the research on nanowires is being done. Imagine the implications of being able to receive the thoughts of others. Would national secrets have any relevance? Would nationalism cease to exist, once we all became a single Worldwide Mind?

Perhaps you can envision how a Worldwide Mind would be structurally similar to becoming One, spiritually, with the universe. It would give you an all-encompassing understanding that all of us are connected all the time. We just rarely realize it.

Ramez Naam, CEO of Apex Nanotechnologies, is one of the leading authorities on the Worldwide Mind concept. He helped develop the Microsoft Internet Explorer and Outlook software, sits on the advisory board of the Institute for Accelerating Change, and is a fellow of the Institute for Ethics and Emerging Technologies. Naam wrote a book called "More than Human: How Technology Will Transform Us and Why We Should Embrace It." He was interviewed on an episode of the PBS television program "22nd Century" that focused on the Worldwide Mind:

NAAM: The idea of the Worldwide Mind is that throughout history, we as a species have created more and more technologies to allow ourselves to communicate with one another. When we first evolved, when we first became human, we could speak. We learned language. That was really the thing that separated humans from the primates that came before us. The next step was when we developed writing several thousand years ago. After writing, we developed the printing press, which made literacy available to many more people. The printing press set off the Renaissance, with the ability to communicate all this information, more and more, between people. People got access to more ideas. They could bounce their ideas off of other ideas. They could build on things. That human brain, that human society, got smarter and smarter.

INTERVIEWER: A collective intelligence of sorts?

NAAM: The human society got smarter and smarter itself. It's like every human being is a neuron, and humanity as a whole is one giant brain. So if you can increase the ability of humans to communicate with each other, to do something like the printing press, or the telephone, or the Web, you make the whole planet smarter.

INTERVIEWER: What's the next step?

NAAM: The ultimate technology for this might be the direct connection of one person's brain to another. For instance, the Worldwide Mind means that you might be able to close your eyes, visualize a scene, and have that communicated to someone else directly, without words, without drawing a picture. You might be able to feel what someone else is feeling. You might be able to share ideas, or emotions, or sights, or sounds directly.

At present, the only known way to connect to the Absolute (the universal consciousness) is through mystical methods like those described in this book. A true Worldwide Mind, with human brains connected by a vast wireless network, would require significant breakthroughs in biology, engineering and cognitive science.

"But as we all know," wrote science journalist Michael Chorost, "equivalent breakthroughs have enabled technologies that our ancestors could not even have imagined. We're like Alexander Graham Bell, the inventor of the telephone, trying to imagine television in the 1870s and predicting how it would change society. He really wouldn't have been able to do it."

Chorost has first-hand knowledge of how a brain's neural network can be interfaced with electronic digital information. He has a cochlear implant in his skull that converts sound waves into signals that his brain can understand as real sounds. Far from a normal hearing aid, which just amplifies sound, this implant actually "speaks" the silent neurological language of the brain.

"I'm a totally deaf man who can use a cell phone," Chorost wrote. "Many eminent scientists and engineers considered the concept of cochlear implant ridiculous in the 1970s. They objected that it wouldn't be possible to get electrodes into the inner ear, that no computers existed that could do the processing in real time, and that no one understood the neural coding of the ear. Do those objections sound just a little bit familiar? They were solved with decades of patient research and engineering. Perhaps the Worldwide Mind idea will take a similar trajectory."

We use the Worldwide Mind example merely to illustrate the concept of the Absolute – the ultimate reality that all things are one. A Worldwide Mind produced by technology would be a simple microcosm or puny mirror of the Absolute, because it would be confined to just one species on one tiny, insignificant planet.

Becoming one with the Absolute is the act of one's consciousness becoming attuned to its connection with everything – the entire universe and everything in it. This is what you experience in the seventh step: Oneness.

While we can demonstrate this mystical concept with the science of the Worldwide Mind, the reality is that one must achieve Oneness through a phenomenon that transcends words, books, lessons and instructional videos. It comes from a "knowing" that is beyond knowledge.

By definition, mysticism is a doctrine which posits that direct knowledge of spiritual truth is attainable through immediate intuition or insight in a way differing from ordinary sense perception or the use of logical reason.

Through meditation and the conscious shutdown of your senses, you are able to "clean the slate" and allow your consciousness to return to its source. By whatever name, that source is the same: Heaven, the Force, Nirvana, Tao, Absolute Bliss Consciousness. When you touch it for the first time, you will know it. We can't guarantee it will match your vision of Heaven; in fact, some people are disoriented or even frightened by the sensation. It's comparable to death; the human consciousness that once defined your sense of self has been replaced by a universal consciousness. You are Everything, but no longer Something.

This is the destination for which you were programmed the moment you entered the step of Balance. The experience of Oneness is impossible to explain adequately with words. It's like trying to describe an orgasm to somebody who has never experienced one. Words can't do it justice. But we are obliged to try.

Once you touch the Absolute, you don't love anymore, and you don't hate. Nothing makes you happy, and nothing makes you sad. Those feelings all belong to the material world. You have detached, and you accept everything as it is. All your motivations from the material world cease to exist. Also, your sense of self is no longer defined by outside sources. If others judge you to be fat, skinny, smart, dumb, beautiful, ugly, lazy or busy, you no longer care. Labels have no meaning in the Absolute. You're not your name, and you're not your profession. "You" don't exist anymore.

You don't feel that you've merely connected to the Absolute. You haven't simply become aware that you are part of the Absolute. You *are* the Absolute. A beggar in the street isn't someone to be pitied, because you *are* the beggar. The President isn't to be judged evil or good – you *are* the President. You are like a drop of water that has fallen into the ocean. The drop no longer exists separately; it *is* the ocean.

You become quiet. Nothingness is enough. You travel within, and you don't want to talk much. Up to this point, you were still debating, always aware that you were going against the flow. You were feeling the weirdness. But now, it doesn't bother you. You're in the dead zone.

You're not human. You could die, and it wouldn't matter. Your senses are gone, and you don't need comforts. You don't focus anymore, you just see. You're flying all over the place. You have completely let go. It's like your meditation has become a permanent trance. You're doing nothing, saying nothing, not convincing anybody. In a flash, all questions are answered for you. Balance is always the solution. This is the inner wisdom, the inner light.

You don't feel the touch of clothes on your body or the chair you might be sitting in, because they're not separate from you. You *are* the chair. People think you're crazy. It's the peak of perfection, exactly like having an orgasm. The universe and you are One, and the only reason you don't have that sense of happiness is because pleasure can't exist without its opposite, and you're incapable of feeling unhappiness. Everything just *is*, and you accept it with a "knowing" that permeates every cell in your body.

Does all this make sense? Of course not. There's no way for anybody to know what the seventh step is like unless they have been there.

For one who has achieved Balance, passed through the steps of Satisfaction and Detachment, then finally attained Oneness, it would seem like there's nothing left to do. You have experienced the Promised Land. It doesn't get any better than this. Why bother doing anything else?

But few who merge with the Absolute stay in that state the rest of their lives. Most dance there for a while, then drop back down to one of the other spiritual levels so they can interact with their fellow beings. Most often, they seem to become teachers so that others may see what they have seen.

During the process, you realized you were different from everybody else. You detached. You were no longer invested in the common pursuits of your fellow men and women. Then, at the level of Oneness, you come back to Earth and realize that if you could share this mystical knowledge, you could help the universe fulfill its natural drive toward Balance. It's not something you *want* to do, because desire is no longer relevant to your existence, but it's something you are drawn toward, as part of the universe's organic tendency to balance itself.

Neal Donner, Ph.D., discussed this tendency of enlightened beings in "Mysticism and the Idea of Freedom: A Libertarian View." He asked: Does this mystic live a life which is for and about himself alone, absorbed in the pursuit of his ecstasy in disregard of the ecstasies of others? Donner wrote:

"There do exist certain libertarians who view any concern for others as a distraction from the sole proper object of attention, which they think to be themselves. Other libertarians accept that no one is completely free unless we are all free. For them, the urge to personal liberation does not sever the bonds of compassion that tie them to other human beings (and often, animals).

"There is a fascinating parallel to this opposition in the history of Buddhism. Around half a millennium after the time of the Buddha (who lived ca. 560-480 B.C.), there arose a new philosophical, and ultimately popular movement, which called itself the Mahayana ('greater vehicle'). Labeling as Hinayana ('lesser vehicle') the earlier forms of Buddhism, which were concerned above all with personal realization, the new movement argued that the highest religious experience (enlightenment, Buddhahood, the mystical experience, etc.) could not be had without simultaneously striving for the enlightenment of others. According to the new teachings, the potential Buddhahood of every other living being had to be acknowledged in order for personal enlightenment to be achieved."

Donner sees no contradiction in striving for the enlightenment of others at the same time as one strives for enlightenment for oneself.

"The apparent contradiction," he says, "is resolved by the awareness of our interconnections with each other, by our dawning knowledge that though we are individuals, paradoxically our destiny is unthinkable apart from other beings."

This matches with your realization at the stage of Oneness that we are not distinctly separate beings. Helping others reach enlightenment is simply keeping yourself in tune with the frequency of the Absolute.

"Those mystics," Donner writes, "who insist that enlightenment requires a radical separation from society, a severing of ties with other humans – a life where compassion, love and shared ecstasy are seen as a distraction from the main quest for enlightenment – are prisoners of a lower understanding. The most resolute pursuit of self-perfection requires a constant awareness of one's interrelationships with others."

We take Donner's conclusion one step further. We believe "others" are merely an illusion of individuality. This book exists because in the ultimate state of Oneness, the Absolute consciousness moves toward Balance.

Chapter Seventeen

TRUTH, REALITY AND
CONSCIOUSNESS

It is your turn now,
you waited, you were patient.
The time has come,
for us to polish you.
We will transform your inner pearl
into a house of fire.
You're a gold mine.
Did you know that,
hidden in the dirt of the earth?
It is your turn now,
to be placed in fire.
Let us cremate your impurities.
Rumi

We touched on an idea in the previous chapter that we'd like to expand upon, because it's important if we are to accept the existence of an Absolute reality that can only be reached by traveling beyond our senses. It's the idea that reality is nothing more than what our brains tell us is real.

In a way, you already know the power of your brain to create its own "reality." Before you ever saw this book, you knew that your brain could tell you there's a lake on the horizon that isn't really there. It's just a mirage, but you see it just the same. Where is the line drawn between perception and reality? The mirage can be proven to be false, but other aspects of "reality" can be a lot more slippery.

The words on this page are visible because of light all around you, but you know that the light is really there only because of an electro-chemical signal that your eye transmits through your optic nerve. These signals travel into the depths of your brain, sealed in total darkness within your skull. Deep inside your visual cortex, in a place where light has never reached, a neuron reacts. And you can see. But what do you see? Whatever your brain tells you. A person with red-green color blindness sees a beautiful lawn, but it doesn't look even remotely like the same lawn that a person with "normal" color vision sees. Both observers know a reality about the color of grass that will never change in their entire lifetime, yet their realities are different. Which one is right? Does the concept of a "right" perception hold any validity?

Differing versions of the same reality can be established for many if not most human perceptions, even when abnormalities like color blindness aren't present. It could be stated that no two people see the world exactly alike. And it's absolutely certain that other species perceive reality in strikingly alien ways.

A fly, with its compound eyes, receives a bizarre, multiple-image version of the world, but nobody really knows how a fly brain processes those signals. Blind bats "see" with echo-location like radar, but do their brains construct a "visual" representation of their world based on sound waves? All we can say for sure is that their reality is very different from ours, and the only reason we think ours is the "real" reality is because we are egocentric humans.

What is reality? "Nobody actually knows, although everyone presumes to know it," writes Giuliana Conforto, Ph.D., astrophysicist and author of "The Organic Universe." She starts with the presumption that human observation is not at all objective...

> "...because it depends on the narrow limits of our perception and, mainly, on the particular theory or cultural system of reference we adopt to interpret our observations.
>
> "No definition of reality or 'objective' matter actually exists, either from a scientific or from a philosophical point of view. According to quantum physics, particles are not objects, but simply wave-functions, i.e., probabilities of being observed.

"Our reality seems to be separated, apparently 'divided' into opposites, such as I and other, human being and environment, matter and spirit, body and mind, science and religion, and so on. Science and particularly quantum physics discovered what sages and philosophers have been affirming for thousands of years, i.e., that we live in an illusion, in a restricted form of perception, which prevents us from awareness of parallel infinite worlds."

Dr. Conforto adds, "Multi-dimensionality and the deep interconnectedness of the cosmos, as well as the interdependence between the I 'subject' and the 'object,' has already been expressed in fundamental principles such as Mach's and the indeterminacy principle."

Reality is a word that's supposed to mean that which is actual or real, as opposed to illusion, but all it can really mean is how we perceive our world. Right now, you perceive yourself to be a solid being who is touching other things, like this book, the clothes on your body, perhaps a chair. But on the level of elementary particles, nothing touches anything. They have electromagnetic charges that repel each other, which means you are actually floating free in space at this very moment, with none of your elementary particles touching any others. Neutrinos traveling close to the speed of light are passing right through you without even touching any of your own personal elementary particles. That's how loosely packed your constituent parts really are.

It all depends on your perspective. If you were the size of a neutrino, the Earth and everything on it wouldn't even seem to exist.

"We normally believe that we see matter, but in reality, we do not," Dr. Conforto wrote.

"We only see the light reflected ... only the visible part of the vast electromagnetic spectrum. If our eyes were sensitive to different wavelengths such as X-rays, we should all appear as skeletons. Buildings would be transparent and subsoil would be visible. All the boundaries would be totally different.

"Different boundaries would also emerge if we could see in infrared wavelengths. 'Reality' critically depends on which specific wavelength we are observing. Transparency, visibility and solidity are qualities which are not intrinsic to the object, but rather to our way of perceiving them."

Our skewed version of reality distracts us from the deeper truth that we are all connected, that all matter is a single, cosmic consciousness.

Dr. Conforto believes "reality" is just a set of interpretations we have made of our world.

"After centuries of restricted and distorted perception, we have collectively developed a dual way of thinking," she writes. "Duality is the conventional way of knowing. It presumes a distinction between the observer and the observed. Therefore, it is the common belief that an 'objective' world exists."

A human mind just naturally accepts this duality – that the universe consists of the individual and everything outside itself. They don't appear to be the same in any measurable way. Science is based on studying "otherness."

When mystics employ altered states of consciousness to probe the Ultimate Reality, they are struck by a revelation: duality is just another illusion. They learn this not from reading a book, but from personal experience. They feel it: Oneness is the deeper truth, and Balance is the driving force of all existence.

Truth and reality can be slippery concepts, and we are told this by the best minds that philosophy and science have to offer. Albert Einstein said, "Reality is merely an illusion, albeit a very persistent one."

Science, and particularly quantum physics, has opened our eyes to how wrong we've been about our perceptions of reality. We are beginning to understand just how much we don't understand.

Philosophers offer a context for our understanding to transcend the rigors of math and science. They open our minds to alternate universes of thought. Religion gives us a perspective that acknowledges a power greater than ourselves. It offers us a way to make sense of our intuitive knowledge that "this isn't all there is." Ultimately, however, it has been our mystics who discovered that consciousness is the key to the kingdom. The elusive concepts of truth and reality can be fully absorbed when one escapes the illusion of duality, reconnects with the Absolute and finds the wisdom and inner peace of Oneness.

What is truth? Historically, the most popular early theory of truth was the Correspondence Theory: Truth is what valid reasoning preserves. It means that X is true if, and only if, X corresponds to a fact, such as "snow is white." The theory breaks down when we learn that snow isn't white unless it's seen under a full spectrum of light.

The Semantic Theory of Truth refines Correspondence Theory, safely saying that, "under given conditions (for example, when seen in sunlight on Earth), snow is white." But the same level of truth can't be claimed for the color of grass to a person with color-blindness. His snow may be white, but his grass won't be green, no matter what kind of light it's seen under. He can't see green. You might argue that the grass is still green, even if the color-blind person can't see it, but color perception, like almost everything else, is relative. Absolute truth remains elusive.

So, philosophers take us on a joyride of truth with their Redundancy Theory of Truth, or the Performative Theory, or the Presentential Theory, and many more. However fun the search for an absolute definition of truth may be, we find no consensus of opinion.

Mathematicians will tell you that truths can be proven. One plus one equals two, and that's a truth you can take to the bank. But mathematicians can't tell you the truth about reality, because their equations will only take you so far. Scientists, with their rigid testing procedures, can prove specific elements about reality on a physical level, but their theories break down in the center of a cosmic black hole or on the quantum level of subatomic particles. Theologians will tell you that truth is revealed by God or the prophets in their scriptures. No proof is needed, because they accept this absolute truth on faith alone.

Our belief is that truth is personal. What's true for you might not be true for another, but that doesn't make it any less true for you.

For example, we believe that you can cure cancer with your mind, just as easily as you can give yourself cancer with your mind. If you don't believe this, it's not true – for you. But our truth is that your health is a direct result of how you react to the conditions in your life. This is not a new idea. Many books have been written about the "mind-body connection," and perhaps the most famous example comes from author Norman Cousins.

Diagnosed with a terminal disease in 1964, Cousins was told by doctors that he would soon die a painful death. He noticed that when he watched a Marx Brothers comedy, his pain eased. So he got every Marx Brothers movie and watched comedy all the time. His immune system soared, and Cousins recovered, living a productive life for 26 more years before dying of heart failure at 75.

The only thing that surprises us about speculation on the mind-body connection is that anyone would ever even doubt that your body is controlled by your mind. It's obvious from the subtle to the severe; from the way embarrassment causes your face to flush, to the way stress causes ulcers and cardiac arrests. The only flaw in the concept of a mind-body connection is that it presumes the mind and body are two separate entities. They're not just connected – they're one and the same. You are a microcosm of the universe – a colony of single-celled organisms working together to form a cohesive whole ... just as the universe itself is a colony of "individual" expressions of the Absolute.

Where does the individual leave off and the cohesive "whole" begin? The distinction between the two is an illusion. We're all part of the One, just as every cell in your body is a part of the whole that is you.

This is a kind of truth that can definitely be expressed by

science or philosophy, but it's most convincing when you experience it first-hand while in an altered state of consciousness, such as one that can be achieved through deep meditation. When touched in this manner, the truth becomes absorbed as inner wisdom. It's a spiritual knowing beyond words, not unlike religious revelation, but more accurately aligned with mysticism. Through consciousness, and consciousness alone, we find our own personal truth and our own personal reality.

Chapter Eighteen

THE LIVING UNIVERSE

*Evolution is a tightly coupled dance, with life and the material
environment as partners. From the dance emerges the entity Gaia.*
James Lovelock

Our world is alive. Not just covered with living organisms. Not
just teeming with life. The Earth itself is a living "creature." This is
the basis of the Gaia Theory, posited by Dr. James Lovelock more
than forty years ago. A British scientist and inventor, Lovelock hit
upon the idea shortly after working with NASA on theories about
life on Mars. The theory gets its name from Gaea, Greek goddess
of the Earth, and mother of Cronus and the Titans in ancient
mythology.

"For me, the personal revelation of Gaia came quite suddenly -
like a flash of enlightenment," Lovelock said.

"I was in a small room on the top floor of a building at the Jet
Propulsion Laboratory in Pasadena, California. It was the
autumn of 1965 ... and I was talking with a colleague, Dian
Hitchcock, about a paper we were preparing. ... It was at that
moment that I glimpsed Gaia. An awesome thought came to
me. The Earth's atmosphere was an extraordinary and unstable
mixture of gases, yet I knew that it was constant in composition
over quite long periods of time. Could it be that life on Earth
not only made the atmosphere, but also regulated it - keeping it
at a constant composition, and at a level favorable for
organisms?"

From that moment of inspiration, Lovelock created a model of our
planet as a single, living, self-regulating system. It adapts to
change and evolves. It lives.

His theory gained credibility with a succession of discoveries over the past several decades. One of the most startling was the evidence that cloud formation isn't just a physical and chemical reaction, but the direct result of life itself. Over the open ocean, cloud formation turns out to be almost entirely a function of the metabolism of oceanic algae that emit large sulfur molecules as waste gases. Those molecules become the condensation nuclei for raindrops.

Cloud formation is vital for our well-being. It not only helps regulate Earth's temperature, but it's also an important mechanism for returning water and sulfur to ecosystems on land. Life maintains conditions suitable for its own survival. The living Earth does the same, thereby enhancing its own survival.

If not for the self-regulating actions of our living planet, global warming would have barbecued us all a long time ago, and it has nothing to do with holes in the ozone layer, hairspray or deodorant.

Our sun is burning almost 30 percent brighter than when life began about 4 billion years ago. But our atmosphere, powered by life itself, adapts and changes enough to keep our surface temperature within that narrow range necessary to sustain our species.

Mother Earth isn't partial to humans, and we don't believe the planet regulates its own systems with intelligence or reason. You can't point to a brain for Mother Earth and say, "That's where she's making all these decisions." Instead, her actions are governed by the same rule that motivates everything and everybody in the entire universe – balance.

Our planet reacts to imbalance by changing. It's constantly striving for greater balance.

Mother Earth is completely unbiased when it comes to balance. If one of her species creates a planetary imbalance by ravaging her own ecology – whether it's caused by human-generated greenhouse gases or the methane flatulence of cows – Mother Earth will react. She'll become a hot and unfriendly place for those species. They'll die out.

Over the eons, balance will return. Imbalance and balance are temporary states, like a pendulum swinging back and forth.

Admittedly, these ideas are still considered to be in the realm of theory. Different levels of Gaia theory exist, from conservative to radical. Most scientists reject the more radical Gaian hypothesis, that the Earth is an organism that undergoes actual homeostasis while balancing its environment. (Homeostasis is an organism's self-regulation of a constant internal state. You're creating homeostasis at this very moment).

Imagining the Earth as a living organism has vague religious connotations, and many people don't like the idea that there's some kind of purpose behind Gaia's actions. We recall the old eco-friendly slogan that warned, "It's not nice to piss off Mother Nature."

Other versions of Gaia avoid the portrayal of a godlike or vengeful planet. The moderate Gaia hypothesis states that the Earth behaves like a living organism, yet isn't actually alive. Most favored is the "weak" Gaia hypothesis, which says that all this apparent homeostasis is governed by negative feedback; when something gets out of balance (like temperature), it's automatically regulated by another process triggered by the imbalance.

After Dr. Lovelock's "eureka" moment in 1965 gave birth to the Gaia theory, it gained traction when the first photographs from space showed the blue planet in its entirety. The national and state borders that everybody saw on maps and globes their entire lives were missing. Intellectually, we knew that would be true, but seeing its reality for the first time led to an epiphany: boundaries are arbitrary and imaginary, and the world truly is a single One. Our first-ever global snapshot showed a complete, integrated and self-regulating system.

But the first seeds for Gaia were planted in human consciousness at least as early in 1929, when Russian scientist V.I. Vernadsky observed that life is part of Earth's own mechanism. "Life appears as a great, permanent and continuous infringer on the chemical 'dead-hardness' of our planet's surface," Vernadsky said. "Life therefore is not an external and accidental development on the terrestrial surface. Rather, it is intimately related to the constitution of the Earth's crust, forms part of its mechanism, and performs in this mechanism functions of paramount importance, without which it would not be able to exist."

So is the Earth really alive? It depends on how you define life. One common definition holds that to be considered alive, an organism must be capable of growth, stimulus response, metabolism, homeostasis, reproduction, adaptation and autonomous motion. Others aren't so strict, pointing out that a mule can't reproduce, yet it's clearly alive.

No single definition of life is accepted by all fields, but one of the most popular definitions came from Chilean neuroscientists Humberto Maturana and Francisco Varela. They said that to qualify as life, an organism must be able to self-produce the components that specify it as a concrete unit in space and time.

By this definition, there's no requirement for life to grow, reproduce or pass on DNA. Since, as Vernadsky observed, 99.9% of the different molecules on Earth have been created in the life process of Earth, the Earth would seem to qualify as a self-making organism.

Mother Earth is definitely producing her own components in a way that seems more alive than any plant or flower (which are also living organisms), but did she create herself, too? If you believe in Creation by the Almighty, the answer might be no – unless you accept that the Almighty is part of the same totality that we call The Absolute. That idea, as well as the Big Bang Theory so widely accepted by science, leads us to an even more radical theory: Not only is Mother Earth alive, but the entire universe is a single, living organism.

Your body is nothing more than a colony of single-celled organisms, but we still define you as an individual living being. In the same way, we believe Gaia (Mother Earth) is a colony of living organisms that work together to "self-produce the components that specify it as a concrete unit." It's alive.

For the next step, imagine your viewpoint is like a camera. You start by focusing on a single white blood cell in a human capillary.

Then your camera zooms out to capture the entire human. Zoom out again, and you see the entire blue planet. Zoom out once more, and you see the entire universe.

Each time you zoomed out, you captured the image of a living "whole" that was comprised of smaller, living individuals. Your cells live. You live. Mother Earth lives. The universe lives.

Most important of all, they are all connected. When the blood cells in your arteries are clogged, your entire body is affected. When humans burn the Brazilian rainforests, the entire Earth is affected. When a star system explodes, the entire universe is affected. This idea is expressed visually in the original "Star Wars" movie, when Darth Vader orders the destruction of the planet Alderaan. As the planet explodes into pieces, the Jedi Master Ob-Wan Kenobi staggers, light-years away, and says, "I felt a great disturbance in the Force, as if millions of voices suddenly cried out in terror and were suddenly silenced. I fear something terrible has happened."

The idea that everything everywhere is connected was expressed much earlier by poet Francis Thompson (1859-1907). Pay particular attention to the last two lines of his verse:

When to the new eyes of thee
All things by immortal power,
Near or far,
Hiddenly
To each other linkéd are,
That thou canst not stir a flower
Without troubling of a star . . .

Evidence of this cosmological interconnectedness is everywhere. As the moon orbits the Earth, its gravitational pull tugs at large bodies of water and creates our tides. The Earth and moon circle the sun, tied by invisible force. Other planets, moons, asteroids and comets join the cosmic carousel, all causing little wiggles in the sun's own rotation because of their gravity.

On a larger level, our solar system rotates in the arm of a vast spiral galaxy we call the Milky Way. Its organization as an immense, interactive system is undeniable.

Only recently have we learned that the connection of astronomical structures continues upward and outward in all directions. Galaxies form clusters, and those form super clusters. In 1989, astronomers uncovered the Great Wall – a sheet of galaxies more than 500 million light-years long and 200 million light-years wide, but only 15 million light-years thick. The existence of this structure escaped notice for so long because it requires locating the position of galaxies in three dimensions.

Astronomers and astrophysicists have learned that if they want to truly understand the structure of the universe, they have to think in multiple dimensions and accept that unseen and poorly understood forces like "dark matter" and gravity link everything together as a whole.

Until our ability to measure, test and prove our theories improves, we are left with "best guesses" as to how it all works. The realms of the scientist, theologian, philosopher and mystic aren't so very different.

Chapter Nineteen

YOUR PRACTICAL GUIDE

*Three favorite rules of thumb: Is the proposed operation likely to
succeed? What might be the consequences of failure? Is it in the realm
of practicality in terms of materiel and supplies?*
Chester Nimitz

We are proposing 7 Steps to Wisdom and Inner Peace that are
traveled by a path of mysticism – a travel within, where your
consciousness reveals truths that books and lectures are incapable
of fully expressing. Is this practical?

To see if it's a worthwhile endeavor, let's use the three favorite
rules-of-thumb of Adm. Chester Nimitz, commander of the U.S.
Pacific Fleet during World War II.

1. Is the proposed operation likely to succeed?
2. What might be the consequences of failure?
3. Is it in the realm of practicality in terms of materiel and
   supplies?

First, if you are sane and capable of reading this deep into the
book, we believe your chances of success are directly proportional
to your level of commitment. If you want it, you shall have it. Your
chances of succeeding are 100 percent.

This is not a difficult road to travel, and success isn't dependent
on effort or unusual mental ability, but merely commitment.
Meditation is a mental discipline, and one must practice to achieve
maximum results. It should be extremely pleasant, enjoyable and
rewarding. If you fail to achieve Oneness and an altered state of
consciousness through meditation, it won't be because you can't
do it, but only because you gave up before you got there.

Some people might connect on their first or second meditative
experience. Others may need many years of study, contemplation

and meditation with masters or gurus before they experience Oneness. It depends on where your "head is at," because that's where the entire journey takes place.

If you believe that all this mystical talk is a bunch of baloney, your chances of failure are probably close to 100 percent. While it's possible for a skeptic to try meditation and stumble into a transcendental experience, it's far more likely that a self-defeating attitude will result in self-defeat. So the answer to Adm. Nimitz's first rule of thumb is yes, the operation is likely to succeed.

What if you fail? The consequences are as critical or as meaningless as you deem them to be. The downside of "failure" is that you will fall somewhere short of Oneness and won't feel you've achieved full wisdom and inner peace. If that's a disaster in your personal life, then you really haven't failed, you just haven't stuck with it long enough to reach your goal. Keep going, and you'll get there. If falling short doesn't really matter to you, then you've lost nothing except the time it took to read this book and try a little meditation.

Falling "somewhere short of Oneness" could mean you reached the elevated state of Detachment, in which you basically left behind all your worldly cares and worries. That can't be called failure. Or what if you stabilize in the level of Satisfaction or Balance? You're living light-years beyond the level of wisdom and inner peace you see in almost everyone around you. That isn't failure, either. The worst that could happen is that you come away from this experience having a little deeper understanding of mysticism, science, religion, philosophy and, most important of all, yourself. So we don't have to worry about the consequences of failure.

Is it practical in terms of materiel and supplies? This is the easiest "yes" of all three rules-of-thumb. Wisdom and inner peace are free. You don't have to invest in expensive meditation lessons or pay a private guru to take you under his wing. You don't need to spend month at the Esalen Institute in Big Sur, California, learning about the seven chakras of biophysical energy or Reiki healing techniques. You don't need to climb a mountain in Tibet to seek guidance from a monk. You *can* do any or all those things if you wish, and they might actually benefit your journey, but none of it is required. The path is a personal one, and as we mentioned in the last chapter, reality and truth are personal perceptions. What works for you is real. Whatever doesn't work can be discarded.

The most significant requirement will be time. If you've never meditated before, it will take time to learn how. And then it will take time to become proficient at it. But the time won't feel like a sacrifice. Instead, you'll find yourself wanting to devote even more of your time to this practice, because it leaves you feeling more relaxed, serene, balanced and happy than usual.

So your journey through the 7 Steps to Wisdom and Inner Peace is practical even by the guidelines of a famous World War II admiral.

Since we're focusing on practicality, let's look at a simple, practical guide to what we're talking about in this book – "How to Achieve Wisdom and Inner Peace." It's as easy and clear as this step-by-step process:

1. Understand and recognize how Wanting, Receiving and Giving have motivated your life's course to this point.
2. Learn about meditation, and experiment with different techniques to see how you can best achieve a deep state of altered consciousness that allows you temporary freedom from your senses and usual brain chatter.
3. Using meditation, continually foster greater Balance in your life by mentally moving beyond Wanting, Receiving and Giving.
4. Use the ever-growing Balance in your life to reach a deep, inner Satisfaction that can't be shaken because you've moved past Wanting, Receiving and Giving.
5. Naturally flow from Satisfaction into Detachment as you intuitively realize that the desires that drive everyone around you are so meaningless that you no longer identify with the society that produced you.

6. Regain your natural birthright, a connection to the universe, as you achieve Oneness through meditation and ever-present wisdom and inner peace.
7. Live the rest of your life with wisdom and inner peace.

From a practical standpoint, it's not realistic to expect you will reach the level of Oneness and stay there forever. If you still have to deal with people and events in the material world, you'll have to "come down from the mountaintop" often. But once you know how to get there, you can return often.

The 7 Steps to Wisdom and Inner Peace also offer a very practical and positive impact on your life: freedom from anger, disappointment, worry, fear and many of the emotions that can send your life into a tailspin. Once you've moved past the first three steps and embraced Balance, you no longer "sweat the small stuff." Occasionally, tragic or catastrophic events may throw you temporarily out of Balance. But because you've been there before, you can find your way back.

Once you reach the level of Satisfaction, events that formerly would upset you seem trivial. The boss who yells at you or the driver who cuts you off in traffic can only make you smile. Anger no longer exists. At the point of Detachment, your worries are over. Your sense of peace and happiness is no longer dependent on outside occurrences. You find your peace within. And when you're finally at One with the universe, you realize "I am he, as you are he, and we are all together." Nothing is separate from yourself. Nothing is accidental or tragic. Everything is what it is. You are totally free from guilt, fear, anger, worry, disappointment – all the negative emotions. You are as one with the gods.

Chapter Twenty

A ROUNDTABLE DISCUSSION

The aim of argument, or of discussion, should not be victory,
but progress.
Joseph Joubert

Do the ideas in this book stand up to scrutiny and challenge by brilliant minds from the worlds of science, philosophy and religion? To put it to the test, my co-author and I brought together an accomplished philosopher, a prominent scientist and an eloquent theologian. Each was asked to read chapters of this manuscript and take part in a frank, roundtable discussion with me and my co-author, who acted as moderator.

Neither the scientist nor philosopher had ever met me before the day of this roundtable discussion, and while the theologian and I had spoken on a few occasions, we were not close, and we certainly did not share the same religious viewpoint. What follows is a verbatim transcript of that discussion, edited only to reduce repetitive or irrelevant tangents.

Our participants:

BOB GASPARINI is President and Chief Science Officer of Neogenomics, Inc., and recognized as a national leader in genetic testing. He's a former adjunct professor at Harvard University and founder of the genetic technology program at the University of Connecticut.

DR. JAMES GARDNER, Ph.D. in Clinical/Community Psychology, earned his B.A. in Philosophy and M.A. in Experimental Psychology. He was a professor at Pepperdine University, Ohio State University, University of Queensland and University of the Witwatersrand in Johannesburg, and is now president and CEO of the Internet Marketing Center of California.

MORRIE GOLCHEH teaches the Kabbalah (a theology of rabbinical origin based on Hebrew scriptures) and Meditation at

Westwood Kehila in Los Angeles. He is chairman of the Persian American Jewish Organization at UCLA, founded Progressive Real Estate in Los Angeles, and is author of book on relationships entitled "Voice of Our Soul Mate." Morrie also produced a five-lecture series called "Searching for the Greatness Within Us."

DAVE CUNNINGHAM, serving as moderator for the discussion, is an award-winning writer and journalist who authored, edited or contributed to 14 novels, non-fiction books and anthologies. His work has appeared in hundreds of magazines and newspapers worldwide.

And I, of course, am JAMSHID HOSSEINI.

Our discussion:

DAVE: The name of the book is "Travel Within: 7 Steps to Wisdom and Inner Peace." You have all read the work or are familiar with the concepts. It's kind of a New Age book, but it's more than that. It's a spiritual self-help book. A New Age book will be on the part of the shelf where people look for books on crystals and pyramid power and geomancy and UFOs and things of that nature. They have a certain type of belief system. Jamshid wants this book to be for everybody, not just those interested in New Age material. So he has chapters on science, religion and philosophy to show that his ideas are based on all three disciplines, and you three represent those disciplines. So what we hope today is that you will challenge him or agree with him, depending on what your honest feelings are. He wants it to stand up to scrutiny.

JAMSHID: I want to tell you how and why I think the way I think, and I like to be challenged.

BOB: If I can't see it, touch it or test it, how do I know it's real? That my perspective, coming from the science arena.

JAMSHID: Yes, and in addition to science, one of the most powerful forces in the world today is religion, and it's easy to see how much influence it has on our civilization. I think it's important to have an understanding of religion, too.

MORRIE: I hope that we don't talk today just with our minds, because our minds can only take us so far. But if you allow your soul to talk, you can be uplifted in a way that goes beyond. The name of your book is "Travel Within," so let the soul that is within come out and speak.

JAMSHID: First, briefly, I want to give you a background of what I believe. I started to think this way after I had this experience of dying.

DAVE: The day you drank cobra venom.

JAMSHID: Yes. And then I followed Rajneesh, and they were teaching me to meditate. We would be told to sit and meditate and not say a word for 10 days. Try that sometime. Not for 10 days, but just sit and say nothing for one day. It will change your life. You see things differently. Fasting and not talking. You are resisting your senses. It was difficult. We got to a point where we had to choose. My master said you are on a bridge, and once you cross this bridge, your life will change. You're not going to be on that other side anymore. You're living in a different world.

DAVE: This was when you had the near-death experience?

JAMSHID: Yes. Our group had four foreigners, Eric from France, Scott from England, me and another Persian. There was this snake, and for five years they were feeding him special food, milk and honey, so the poison would not kill. I drank that poison. I went through the fear and saw the white dot of light. I could resist no longer, so I gave up and surrendered. As soon as I did, the whole world was perfect. "Wow, this is beautiful, why would I ever want to go back?" Then I thought about my family and the girl I loved and felt concern for them if I never came back, so I decided to come back and started rejoining the world. I was in that semiconscious state for days. During that time, the whole world seemed different. That's when I started to think and put together all these elements of the 7 Steps to Wisdom and Inner Peace. I came up with this philosophy about how the universe is made, and it allows you to see yourself more clearly. The key is to escape from your senses.

DAVE: Can you elaborate on that?

JAMSHID: It was described to me this way: You learn how to drive. You sit in the driver's seat, and after five, 10 or 20 years, you drive this car without thinking about it. It's all subconscious. The part of you that can drive the car without thinking about it is always inside you. It has always been there. The only way you can let that part out is to somehow get rid of your senses. This is the name of the game. Once you get rid of your senses, you allow that inner driver to take over. This is what religion tries to do. Basically, you have faith in that inner driver. You surrender and have faith that driver will take you in the right direction. If you are able to do that, then you've got it made. This is the philosophy of the book. We are all part of nature, and nature is made of three things: source, anti-source and what I call the axis. Right in the middle of these three things, at the time of the Big Bang, the source experienced the anti-source and started to not be the source anymore. Originally, our source had no location or time.

MORRIE: What is the anti-source?

JAMSHID: It's energy, positive and negative energy, matter and anti-matter, whatever you want to name it. You need to have these elements for anything to exist.

MORRIE: And where did this idea come from? This is Buddhism?

JAMSHID: No, this is mine.

MORRIE: And how did you discover this?

JAMSHID: By seeing it myself, after all that I have lived and seen and done. Because I am made of these elements. Immediately after these three elements came together, everything else started to emerge and change. Everything started to change, always trying to regain that balance.

MORRIE: If you are trying to put these ideas down in a book, I think the most important thing is that the readers are not lost in the process. Once there is a disconnect and the reader cannot see where you're going, you lose them.

JAMSHID: If you let me go to the end and see what I see, then you'll see the science, religion and philosophy. It started at the Big Bang with three things, the source, the anti-source and this axis. If you take out the negative or the positive or the axis, it doesn't exist. You have a force from the source pushing one way and a force from the anti-source pushing the other way. As it was rotating on the axis, this got to a point where it had absolute balance between source and anti-source. Once the source and anti-source collided, everything was out of balance. And because everything moves toward balance, every source will create an anti-source, and every anti-source will create a source, so they can become balanced. It's the same principle of cells splitting. One becomes two, two become four, four become eight, and on and on. The amount of energy in each particle remains the same. Particles react to changes in their environment in ways to maintain balance. So one particle becomes an orange tree, another becomes an ant, another becomes a human being, based on their need for balance. And every single particle in the universe has the memory of Creation. Its mold is stamped on the source. Every single particle in the universe is connected by that common beginning. And every single particle and collection of particles – like human beings and plants and galaxies – is naturally guided toward greater balance. Gravity is a force coming from the anti-source that pushes everything toward greater balance, toward the environment it belongs in, based on the source and anti-source within it.

DAVE: We need to see how this applies to wisdom and inner peace.

JAMSHID: These are the 7 steps. It's the journey from a state of unbalance to becoming balanced. Of course, there are many stops along the way, but there are seven key steps. It has to be an odd number. It has to have a middle. Every step has its own characteristics. The reason I describe it like this is because I believe everything belongs to the physical world. Even the feelings you have create a physical reaction, a direct chemical reaction. When you are a religious or spiritual person, you are more balanced chemically.

JAMES: I don't see how any of these things are related. I don't see how the picture you're drawing is related to your seven steps. Does this all tie in somehow?

DAVE: Obviously, these people have questions. Can we go to the questions now?

JAMSHID: Definitely, we can go to the questions, but you are talking about the 7 Steps, and these are the seven most important experiences that these particles have in order to create me.

BOB: This could be a full-day symposium. From my perspective, which is more quantitative than qualitative, I think I understand what you're saying. What you're describing is something that Einstein has actually quantitated, and that is there is matter – I don't know much about the ionosphere or even much about gravity, other than some of the simple formulas – but I understand what you're saying. There's a push-pull or a yin-yang. There's balance. There's balance in the universe, and it just didn't happen, we evolved to it. But as I think about evolution, a scientist asked, how did we get to be who we are? How did we get to be the height we are, with the intelligence we have, the skin tone we have, the muscle mass we have? The answers to those questions are somewhat quantifiable. We are who we are and got to be who we are because of the potential that got unlocked in the genes that we inherited. Now, many of those genes or at least pieces of those genes can be traced all the way back to the first humans. The question is, you're going even further back, because even life on this planet is a relatively new phenomenon compared to the billions of years. And my sense is that you're talking about how this balance and harmony of energy predates that. My challenge would be, how did we get to where we are now? What was it in the Big Bang theory you mentioned that got us to this point? Is it intelligent design vs. random choice in years of trial and error, and in the evolution of things, how do we tap into these 7 Steps? I'm not even sure my questions are connected.

JASHID: I understand you perfectly.

BOB: How do they layer on? How do they overlap?

JAMSHID: I believe there is nothing in the universe that is beyond our understanding or out of the physical world. Everything is physical. Everything. I would just ask you, what is the biggest secret to survival, or to our existence? What do you think it would be? The most important rule?

BOB: The key to survival? Oxygen? Or you mean balance, I guess?

JAMSHID: Right, it's balance. That's it.

BOB: Balance in everything. I would agree, Jamshid, with the concept of balance, from work to life to growth to death. Balance.

JAMSHID: And it's a dynamic balance. It's a question of imbalance leading to a different kind of balance.

DAVE: It's constantly in flux, is what you're saying.

JAMES: It's in flux, and it's changing. It's like Toynbee's theory of history. It's true those events come back and reformulate, but it's spiraling rather than simply balancing. It's ever-changing even when you bring yourself back into balance. So it's a constant balancing and re-balancing.

DAVE: That brings up a good question, then. If the goal is balance, and in these 7 Steps we get balanced, things are constantly changing in our lives. So how do you stay balanced?

JAMSHID: I have another question I want to answer, and then I will get to that. Look at this universe. It's made of billions of moving particles. Is it just a major accident that the universe is the way we find it today? There's no accident. What law are they following?

BOB: Are you asking, why do we continue to exist? Why does the Earth continue to spin on its axis?

JAMSHID: Simple. In order for a human to exist on Earth, look what we've created. When I leased a building maybe 15 years ago, my lease agreement was three pages. I leased a building for my wife a few days ago, and they gave me about 400 pages. OK? In order for our civilization to exist, the way we are going, you need to have rules and regulations, and it's not getting simpler.

BOB: Things always get more complicated. More layers.

JAMSHID: OK. So therefore, the simpler the existence, the easier it is to exist. The universe has one rule. Only one rule, and nothing else. Everything else is a creation of our minds. The universe says, "Be balanced." Doesn't matter where in the universe you exist. If you're balanced on your axis, you've got it made. It's not any more complicated than that. If you eat food that makes you more balanced, you're more balanced. If you're a religious person, you follow certain rules, and you become balanced. Everything in your body becomes balanced. There's nothing weird about it.

BOB: How would a philosopher approach that, though? The influences on this balance – the physical – are ones we can touch, describe or feel. What about those that we can't? How do you account for the influences of those? What about time and space? Einstein said there's another continuum out there, and perhaps there are parallel universes. Things that exist in time and space that we don't see or feel. Do those play a role?

JAMES: When you're talking about balance, you're talking about one perspective. But in fact, that macro perspective is probably made up of lots of imbalances. There's one here and one there, and those create the next level of balance, but the only reason there's a balance there is because there's an imbalance somewhere else. So balance is a tricky concept.

JAMSHID: To get back to your question of why we are like this: We are made of many elements. Some of them are perfectly balanced and some are not so perfectly balanced. But why are we like this?

JAMES: We are like this because if we weren't like this, we couldn't ask the question, "Why are we like this?"

BOB: The term we use in sentient. We recognize we exist, whereas most animals, anything below homo sapiens, do not.

JAMES: Well, that's debatable, too.

BOB: Because we don't have any way to measure.

JAMSHID: Yeah, what is existence?

MORRIE: Aside from the physical existence? There's a wall there, and that's a real wall, and what I see is really an impression of that real wall. Kabbalah is based on 10 steps and says every completion goes through those 10 steps. It says in the third step, *Keter*, which means crown, that we don't see who's wearing the crown. It's a thought. So everything begins with a thought. And the last step is *Malchut*, which means Kingdom, and Kingdom is the life we live in. Everyone is supposed to be living like a king. And it all begins with a thought. Even that thought can be outside you or perhaps so deep inside you that you need to discover it. That's the kind of thought you're talking about. It's a spiritual thing. You and I and everyone at this table will be absolutely nothing if our life does not have thought, ideas, visions. This is so important. All these things are spiritual. Can you show me an idea? Can you show me a thought? But anybody who has any life worth living has ideas and visions. The bottom line, the physicality we all have, that we can measure, is only because it started somewhere, but you cannot measure or see that. This is how physical and spiritual come together to make a perfect life. OK? I said that last step is *Malchut*, which means Kingdom.

JAMSHID: Same as death, like dying to one's senses. Or Oneness?

MORRIE: Exactly.

JAMSHID: It's the same as death and the same as Oneness and same as balance.

MORRIE: What I want to tell you, and I hope you sell this book, but if I'm doing all these steps to die, because there's death at the end, it's not a very sexy idea. I do all of this to get to death? Death has a negative connotation. It means different things to different people, but if you want this book to be commercially successful, that needs to change. I'm not talking about your other concepts.

JAMSHID: When I say death, I mean death to one's five senses, which is how you achieve Oneness. In the end, nothing dies. There is no death.

MORRIE: I agree 100 percent with you.

BOB: We exist in a different state.

MORRIE: Exactly.

BOB: But people don't want to buy a book telling them how to get there – wherever there is – if you have to die to get there.

MORRIE: It's parallel to what Osama bin Laden said. He said the difference between us and the western people is that they are living to live, and we are living to die. You need to be very careful about these things.

JAMSHID: What do you think life is, and who do you think you are, as a human? I mean, if you look at this universe, how big is the Earth in comparison? And me, sitting here, I'm less significant than an ant to an elephant. When you say death, first of all, nothing dies. But in a human civilization, death has a certain meaning. Just think what happens to you. The only thing that happens is that the electrical connections in your body are disconnected. But do your particles go somewhere out of this universe? No. Every single cell in your body has its own memory, its own experience, its own DNA. In combination, they are all you. Once you die, the only thing that happens is that instead of being one Morrie, there are billions of particles that have the Morrie experience in them. And where do they go? They go to where they are allowed to be, based on physical energy. It's not what you call Heaven with beautiful gardens.

DAVE: What happens when we die is a question that has been examined by science, philosophy and religion. Jamshid says he "died" and came back with a vision of oneness. What do the rest of you think happens when we die?

BOB: I have a couple of short comments. We can "science" away the white lights, the pinpoint of white light you saw in your near-death experience, as the phenomenon of brain cells dying, or in particular, neurons firing and an impression of light forming on the back of your optic nerve. There are scientific hypotheses, difficult to prove but at least grounded in fact, that explain the light we see and the concerns you thought about. We know where in the brain memory is stored, and that's one of the first areas to start to die. And the hypothesis is that those memories are released. I'm not an expert in this area, but it would appear that the light that you saw and the memories you had when you thought you were dying were just cells releasing energy. We still don't understand what it is or where it's going, other than back into the universe. But there may be scientific explanations why people in near-death experiences perceive what they perceive.

MORRIE: I could tell you volumes on this, but from the Jewish perspective, God did not want to create this world. What you see, all the universe, God has created, and God was so good, giving so much, that man's soul was eating the bread of shame, after receiving all this. "I'm not giving, and what can I give to God who has everything?" So there came a need for God to take care of the need of the soul, and the world was created to put the soul in here, and the soul would be each and every one of us, and the soul would come to do something in this world, and because of what we do, we become a creature of God, and later we become part of God, and then there is no more bread of shame, and we are reaping our reward for what we have done in this universe. And every human being is born for three reasons. The first is to make a choice, the second is to be a cause and effect, and third, whatever we get, we must share in love. Underlying all three reasons is joy, because God wanted the soul to be joyous, and because the joyous soul wasn't complete, he created this whole world to complete it. Understanding this is understanding why we came into this life. And what happens when we go back? When we go back, there is no Hell. Because a Cause who is endlessly good could not create Hell, and that burning, painful place is a contradiction to God. Either you believe in God or you believe in Hell. You cannot believe in both. But in Judaism there is a concept known as *Gehenom*, which translates to Hell, but it really doesn't mean Hell. It means a purification process. You wear your clothing, and in the process of wearing, it becomes dirty, so you put it in a washing machine, which is hell for that clothing, but the outcome is clean clothing. We are all going back to God and will be joyous for what we have achieved.

DAVE: From a philosophical point of view, James, what happens when we die, and how do you know it?

JAMES: By the way, Gehenom is a suburb of Jerusalem. There are some religions that believe this world we live in is Hell. This right here. And when we discover that God is inside of us, a part of us that releases us from Hell, then we go back to life. So it's the same concept.

MORRIE: But this is the place where we achieve everything. And it's a privilege, life is a complete privilege. It's important to call it a privilege and not Hell, because in Torah, it says I put life and death in front of you, and I choose life. Sometimes it sounds like a stupid statement. Of course, I would choose life. But you have philosophers who say death is better than life, so let's choose death. Life is a privilege.

JAMES: Some people will choose death if their pain is too great.

MORRIE: That's wrong. Because God is endlessly merciful and would not let someone suffer. He's not sadistic. It's only because we need the pain for a greater purpose of elevation. So if you have pain, you could say, "There is no God, for how would a merciful God give me pain?" That's one philosophy. The other is that you could say, "I'm suffering because God wants me to suffer." That's another philosophy, but what Kabbalah teaches is that if you have pain, there is only one reason: because you need this pain to elevate. There is some message in the pain that you need to get to elevate your soul from the pain. If someone commits suicide because of their pain, they are not allowed to be buried in a Jewish cemetery, because they have cut themselves off from the whole system. The system is, "You're part of God, God is endlessly merciful, whatever happens, there's a message. Do not cut yourself off from this message."

JAMES: How merciful is a God who will let me suffer so much pain that I kill myself, and then he excludes me from his Heaven? This doesn't sound like a merciful God.

DAVE: It's a good question, but we're starting to stray from our point. I'd like to ask each of you the question that Jamshid has spent most of his adult life trying to answer, which is, what is the key to wisdom and inner peace?

MORRIE: Wisdom is accepting there's a greater plan, and you will be happy with wherever you are. And from wherever you are, you grow. I would say, wherever all of this goes, if it's creating a better life for me, it's good, it works. If it does not, it's a waste of time. So life has parts. The word Jerusalem is made of two words. *Jeru* means I will see, and *shalom* is peace. I will see more challenges, difficulties. There will be challenges, and I'm ready, I will embrace challenges, but with *shalom*, with peace.

BOB: I don't mind putting my chips on balance. The Freudian perspective, which is a large part of western thought nowadays, believes you have these competing forces between what you want and what society wants you to do, and you have to balance those two so all energies come to the core and are available for problem-solving in the here and now. Whether you cut it in Freud's cake or Jamshid's cake with the 7 steps, it's a good perspective.

DAVE: So it truly is a question of balance, perhaps?

BOB: I live in a world on the professional side that doesn't think about or deal with these questions. I live in a world that is a mechanism to solve puzzles, so one of the biggest shortcomings of science – and perhaps therein lies one of its greatest strengths – is that when questions need to be answered, we answer those questions, and we don't have to consider the outcomes. The utilization of technologies that we develop at the cutting edge are for the philosophers and theologians, and quite frankly the politicians, to make decisions on. And so I'm probably a little out of my league answering questions about the road to inner peace and wisdom, but science answers a lot of questions on the superficial level. We're not going to get the answers that you seek to impart in this book from a more complete understanding of science. I think it would be silly of us to think that we're the only sentient beings in the universe, although religion might say that we are. It's a statistical certainty that there are other planets like ours. We know that. But are their beings carbon-based? Whatever they might be based on, do they think? Do they believe? On a more personal level, shaped by my 30 years in hard-core science, I believe you need to be able to effect balance. It's all about balance. It's about not doing too much of one thing to excess. I think it's very difficult when you're young to be balanced, because there's so much commotion and distraction and things to do. And I think if there's a target audience that could benefit most from this, it would be the younger. Because I think as we get older, we realize what's more important, and we understand the concept of balance. When we're younger, it's just lip service. It's just a word and not a philosophy. As you get older, you realize true satisfaction comes from your family, from giving as opposed to receiving, and being able to do what contributes to the feeling of inner peace.

JAMES: It's not so much balance, but being in balance. In the same way someone goes across a balance beam. They're never really in complete balance because they're constantly in motion, but the goal of the motion is always to be in balance. So it's not the balance itself, which would imply somebody stood there perfectly balanced, but that we go through life constantly moving forward, pursuing balance.

DAVE: Once you're in balance, and you're in Step 7, how do you maintain that balance when everything is always trying to throw you out of balance?

JAMSHID: If you look at ourselves, you see all decisions are based on two different pressures. There's a duality inside that helps me make decisions. One of those is "real world," what I have to deal with right now. It exists, and I need to take care of it. The other pressure is from what needs to be, and that's the internal program inside, forcing me toward balance. It's in my nature. Sometimes they push you in opposite directions. When you go to become a monk and sit in a temple with nothing to distract you, nobody comes in, the environment is quiet, and it's not difficult to stay focused. But living in the real world makes it very difficult to get past the fourth step. That's why the first three steps are absolutely, totally physical, and you have to train your feelings to go toward the direction that helps you become balanced. Once you go through the fourth step, already you've gone through these steps of having, and learning how to have, and becoming balanced. That's the end of the material world and the steps you can apply to your regular life. You pass that and go to the area of the spiritual world. As I said, you have to disconnect from this world. You have a choice. Either you have to go sit in a temple and never come back, or you live in the real world, where you have this challenge, because you're living, and your feelings are there, and you might find something you have no experience with. But there are always endless possibilities for distractions in our environment to pull you in and out. It's basically your choice.

MORRIE: You say when you reach a state of satisfaction, you go to disconnection. I think I understand where you're going with the disconnect, and a lot of great people in the world have done that, but you know what? When they disconnect, their lives become more within themselves. And they're not addressing the third reason we are all born for, and that is sharing. So another possible thing is that when you get to total satisfaction, you really get so filled with love inside, you want to connect with everyone else. And when I'm so happy inside, I want to hold all of you, and when I come back, I want all of you to be at the stage that I am at, and I want all of us to experience oneness. So it's not going to be disconnection, it's going to be oneness.

JAMSHID: That's a good way of looking at it, but when you pass this fourth step, which is balance, you no longer belong to human life as we know it. You don't belong to this civilization. And at the end of the day, every single particle in this universe has a mission: to become balanced. And you're an individual. This is your mission. If you want to stay and share it with everybody, that's great, but you're not going to achieve those final steps, the spiritual steps, in any other way. I believe it is impossible to have and to be. You either can have or you can be. This is my perspective.

MORRIE: Why can I not have and be? You have this room, and you can also be in this room. You have it, and you're in it.

JAMSHID: There's a major problem with having. I loved to have, every single one of us wants to have as much as we can get. But there is a major problem with that. Having is endless. You need so many rules and regulations to support our having that eventually it's going to destroy us. It's against the mission of our goal. The mission is to become balanced. Why do we become unbalanced?

MORRIE: You are born with ego, and to have things ... wanting is exactly what God has created for you. Imagine this table filled with food and drink and all beautiful things. And you tell us, "Please have some." "No, thank you. We don't want to have anything." You would not be happy. If you own a company with a thousand people, and you want to move on, you are not going to be able to find someone to take the helm of the company if he doesn't want to have anything. God created the world in six days, and it was very good, and Kabbalah says what was very good was the sense of wanting to have things. To want to have things is natural. All of us got out of bed today because we wanted to have something. Otherwise, none of us would be here. To want to have is great. The huge problem is, what do you want to do once you have it? If you just want to have more and more and more, that's destruction. But the beauty of life, the first law of creation, is that we were created to make choices. In order to have a choice, we have natural desires and wants, and what we do with that is up to us.

JAMES: This is not meant to be disrespectful nor grandiose, though goodness knows I've been accused of both, but I think those are more elementary levels. I know in my own life, the last couple years, I go down to Brazil where I help protect the farms. I do that because it's the right thing to do. I don't get much out of it. I spend time rescuing animals, and I do it because it's a good thing to do, and I do it dispassionately. It's not like I feel an urgent need to save some trees or rescue an animal. It's another level, more blissful and more peaceful.

MORRIE: Absolutely, but where is the contradiction between what you said and what I said?

JAMES: Because it's not like I want to have the biggest rain forest preserve or this or that. I have almost no wants. It's just a need I perceived in the world, and that was I slot I could fill. Same with the animal stuff I do. It's just a need I could fill.

MORRIE: This is exactly an application of what I said. You have gotten to this stage, and you're doing that because it's right. This is where the freedom of choice has taken you. You could have said, I want to have this whole forest because I want to own it.

JAMES: Because I want to sell trees or —

MORRIE: Yes, this is exactly what I'm saying. Everything we do has to have a choice in it.

JAMES: And I think what Jamshid calls "disconnect," there's a certain disconnect in doing those things, and it's different from having a mortgage company where I made lots of money, or having an Internet marketing company where I made lots of money, or being a teacher at a university where I could have sex with lots of pretty girls. These are different kinds of things. I'm protecting the forest. And it's disconnected from what normally were my motivators in the past. This is a new kind of behavior.

MORRIE: Do you call it a disconnect, in his case, or do you call it a oneness? To me, you reached a great love in you, and now you're coming back and becoming one with the animals and the forest. The question is, do you call it oneness with the universe or a disconnection?

JAMSHID: Let me tell you one thing to make this very clear in everyday life. We have global warming now, we hear it in the news, it's a serious trend, and we have weird weather. We are destroying ourselves. This world will not be fit for us to live in. The simple law of nature is that the organism has to survive, and I have to be balanced. In order to be balanced, I can't have. Having leads to big problems. It leads to destroying your environment. It takes enormous amounts of energy to satisfy everyone's need to have. If I want to have, and he's standing in my way, I have to get him out of my way so I can have more. There's friction. The desire to have escalates. First you want a car, then you want a Ferrari. You want a house, then you want a castle. How do I acquire these things? I use up energy, a tremendous amount of energy. And along the way, we destroy the Earth, and we destroy each other.

MORRIE: I agree with you. That world will destroy itself.

DAVE: If you get to the point in the 7 steps where you no longer desire, it seems like you are no longer motivated. What would happen to the world of science if nobody wanted, if they didn't desire to find a cure for cancer?

BOB: We do what we do because there are questions to be answered or puzzles to be solved. We don't do it with consequences in mind. We do it for the simple or complex challenge. The academic question to be answered, the secret to be revealed.

JAMES: That's a little too cute. You do it because the federal government decided they are going to sponsor a project. All the years I taught in college, there were very few academics who pursued something for pure altruism, as much as, given they already had an interest, they went where the money was.

BOB: Right. Yes.

JAMES: And somebody had an agenda.

BOB: There is basic research, and most of the basic research in my company is federally initiated or driven. But not all of it. And there are thinkers, people who think up solutions or parameters of boxes that need to be filled in. But the questions that get asked are usually broad, and the answers tend to be specific. So, are they all funded by the government? No. But you're right, we are pushed in the direction of, let's say, cardiovascular disease or cancer. Why? Because of the impact on our life. They shorten our life. And so we get asked questions about why, so ultimately we can do something to prolong our life.

MORRIE: Life couldn't exist if there wasn't wanting.

JAMSHID: Probably this is a good point to make right now. Evolution didn't happen over just a few years. We are changing as we go, even right now. As we go, based on the 7 Steps, these things are part of us, part of our DNA. For example, the area of having, we are born with it. You have to develop the areas that are not programmed in us. You ask, what would society be like when nobody wants to have anymore? First of all, we are going to be forced to get there, as I see it. We're not going to be able to use as much energy as we want to use. And when we get there, you're not just living as an individual, and there's not a moment when you don't have satisfaction. Every single moment, when you are there, is absolutely beautiful. You're happy, you don't have anything that can destroy your happiness. You're living in a perfect world. But if having and wanting are part of your life, you're never going to get there. You have to get past those steps.

DAVE: What really is hard-wired into our DNA? Is a drive for happiness or balance there, or is it just whether you're going to have blue eyes or brown hair?

BOB: The short answer a few years ago would be that the DNA carries only the non-emotional – the eye color, the hair color, IQ. What we're beginning to understand is this potential built within the DNA that spills over into the emotional, and perhaps emotion can even be quantitated in terms of brain chemistry and hormones and enzymes. I think where we're at right now is that it's environmentally influenced. That's the nurturing or non-nurturing environment you're brought up in. Some would say we have the history of the ages in our DNA and the genes. Now, genes themselves have evolved, and they mutate, and we have this fancy term called selective advantage, and many of the gene mutations are beneficial, or at least some are. Many are deleterious, but they're usually weeded out within a few generations. So if the question is, how much is hard-wired and how much is influenced, I don't know that we can quantitate the number. No one really can. We don't have the tools to measure. What we can see are similarities by studying generations, twins, where the genetics are similar. So I wouldn't disagree with what you said. There is an awful lot within our DNA that we don't know. There's more in there that we don't know about than what we do know about. And mostly what we do know about is the structure itself, as opposed to the more complex interactions and even positioning of those genes and the interaction with the environment.

MORRIE: Bob, if I have certain genes, I would pass them along to my children, right?

BOB: Yes.

MORRIE: So let's say during my lifetime, I had no education. At the age of 40, I started studying, and the next 40 years I study and become a learned man. Would my DNA be any different at 80 than when I was 40?

BOB: No, but whatever it was in your DNA that motivated you to go and do what you did at age 40 would be the same potential that you could pass on to your next generations.

DAVE: In the chapter in religion, Jamshid points out that even before recorded history, mankind has gravitated toward a belief in an afterlife and a higher power. Is this in our genes? Is it part of our collective psychology, a need to believe, or is it because it's true?

JAMES: Are you familiar with the theory of the Primal Horde? It was used by Freud, who himself was interested in religion and anthropology. His idea for how these things originated was that back 50,000 years ago, a tribe was ruled by a strong man. And you see examples of it in mammal and primate groups today. The strong man kept the best food and sex for himself, and at some point, as you see in lion and hyena groups, the other young males eventually get fed up with living on the scraps and not having sex, and they're all sitting around one day and decide, "We're going to kill this guy." So they kill the strong man, and they have sex with the females and share all the good food and party for weeks, and eventually they come to a situation where somebody has to organize a hunt. But nobody knows how to do that, because that's what the strong man did. So a whole period of civil unrest ensues, civil wars, as brothers jockey for position. Finally, the women are sick of being raped and not having food, so they set up a matriarchy, and they begin to rule, as you see often in the animal kingdom. According to Freud, this happened over several generations, and at some point, people sit around and say, "Remember those good old days when things used to be right?" And in their myths and totems, they develop the memory of the time when there was a powerful chief who could control everything. Over generations, that became God. I think that's a reasonable theory. In the face of chaos and their desire for order, people believe that somewhere down the line, there's a story that there used to be order.

MORRIE: I have a question for you. When we came into this room, we didn't know each other. We see this beautiful table, walls painted, curtains hanging, and I would ask you a question. How did this come about? Would you say someone set this up? Someone built this building and set up this table?

JAMES: Yes.

MORRIE: OK, it is so elementary that when we see the sun and moon and this endless cosmos, wouldn't you think someone has created this, someone greater than the chief of a tribe who organized the hunt and who became a god? Isn't that something to almost laugh at? Just look at this universe. The word *Emuna* in Hebrew is translated as belief, but it doesn't mean belief. There is no word in Hebrew for belief. It means trust, meaning that you don't believe in God, you trust God. My mind is always boggled by how scientists could not believe in God because you believe every action has to have a cause. You know the sun is going to shine tomorrow, you know all these things about the universe, and not you or I or anyone else could create such a system so perfectly. And your body and my body and the baby in the womb, you see endless miracles every day. And by the way, I don't like the word religion, because religion is such a narrow way to see God. People like Freud who come up with these stories about religion, they really ridicule God. Science is a miracle, too.

BOB: There was a series of books by the author Jean Auel, the Earth's Children series, where the term she used was memories. Memories from the clan. Nowadays we call it instinct. The instincts of fight or flight. The ability of the hippocampus to fire a shot of adrenaline when faced with a dangerous situation. You hear of the hair on the back of your neck rising. There's some science behind that. But these are things that we have evolved from vestigial organs or vestigial senses, so I think the concept of instinct is that there are things, whether they're feelings or action or reactions, that can be passed through your genes or your DNA, as well as the traits we know of. The other thing, and that's Morrie's point, is that we're too complicated a being to have evolved. At least, that's one of the scientific hypotheses right now. Four or five billion years is not enough to lead to the complexity of the human brain or the complexity of the human eye. Science is very careful when it comes to crossing over into religion, but one theory over the last few years is that there must have been intelligent design. We're too complicated a being. Our metabolic and biochemical pathways are so extraordinarily complex, and then when you look at the regulation behind those metabolic pathways – the genes and the interaction of the genes behind that, the control, the regulation – it's too complex to have evolved. There had to have been a being or a god or an intelligent design behind the origin of man. And so I think what you're seeing for the first time now is science trying to quantitate the bridge between religion and science. And I think we'll see more of that. We know what evolution can do, and we understand that five billion years, the age of this planet, is an awful long time, but human beings have only been around, what, 20,000 years or so? You just can't get from there to us and say it was completely evolution.

JAMSHID: I want to tell you a simple practice you can do, as far as God goes, because I believe that what we call God is something that helps us control the power. But who's sitting in the driver's seat? We transfer the power of controlling our environment to the Creator, and we don't to go deep into the question of who the Creator is. But try this simple practice that anybody can do. Find something, a symbol. Take that bowl, for instance. Believe that that's the only bowl on Earth, and it can do everything for you. Put it in a corner and make it nice and clean. Every time you go to the bowl, shower first and wear fine clothes and go in and just sit there, and pray to that bowl. Ask that bowl to control your life. Tell that bowl, "I am nothing, you are everything." Just do this for 30 or 40 days. It will have the exact same effect as the religious God that people believe in. The object of this game is to show you that you must take the control away from this bowl and give it to the big driver inside that has created you. That word God, the bigger and more important it is, the harder it is to deny it. That's why they make it so big. There's a simple rule which governs everything that exists. "Be balanced." If it were otherwise, this universe wouldn't exist as it does. Be balanced. Being balanced doesn't mean you never change. It means you are always changing. The world around you is always changing, and to remain balanced, you have to change with it. Humans used to be covered with hair, but conditions changed, and we changed with it. Now we don't have so much hair. Maybe our ancestors will all be bald. That is Godlike. We change in order to stay balanced with our environment. That's evolution.

MORRIE: In Torah, it talks about false prophets. And if it's a false prophet, how come you don't say, "Charlatans! Liars!" When you say this bowl, if you believe in it, it will do things for you, it's absolutely true. If you believe in it, it will. But you're a false prophet to think it's really the bowl that's doing it. So yes, you could believe in anything you want, and it will work for you, but this is not it.

JAMSHID: It would work for everybody. The end result is the same.

MORRIE: It's not the same. That's exactly my point. It's not the same. Because now you're limited. When the bowl is your thing, you're limited. When your mind is as vast as the whole universe, you're not limited. This is why Talmud says if you kill one person, it's as if you kill the whole world. Your mind is as vast as the whole universe.

JAMSHID: Yes, but you're fighting it. You're fighting against having that universal mind. You're transferring the power to something else.

MORRIE: I say, do not limit yourself to the bowl. If you put your trust in a bowl, you're limited to the bowl.

JAMSHID: It works physically. You play with your mind, you deceive your mind by telling it to believe in the bowl. It's the same principle when you tell your mind to believe in a controlling God outside your body.

MORRIE: No, it isn't. If you want to be like him, the scientist, or if you want to be a homeless man in the streets, you have two different paths. I'm not saying one is right and the other wrong, but they are two different paths, and they will not take you to the same place.

JAMSHID: I just don't look at it as that complicated.

JAMES: I think the history of religion is such that you'd have to say being very religious takes you to a very good place.

MORRIE: I agree with you. That's why I don't like this word religion. What happened is that a lot of people with their own limitations and problems come and bring it to religion, and they paint this spirituality of their religion as limiting. That becomes the bowl. A lot of religion is just like the bowl that he's talking about. And I'm saying no, it's not a bowl. Whatever you say is "it," is not it. Because it's greater than that. It's not limited by man's concepts.

JAMES: If it's my God, it's such a short step from worshipping my God to wanting to destroy everybody who doesn't share that God. Every religious group eventually takes that step.

MORRIE: That's not true.

JAMES: Including the Hebrews when they had the chance.

MORRIE: Absolutely not.

JAMES: They slaughtered everybody. In Jerusalem, Canaan, Sumer. They had hundreds of years slaughtering all those tribes.

MORRIE: No, no, that's so wrong. There is one time that they killed, which was the father, Jacob. It was very harsh, he said you two brothers, you should never be together, because when you're together, you're trouble. Because they're both wanting to receive. When you put together a group of people all wanting to receive, all wanting to take, take, take, the system breaks down. Every system should have give and take so that there's balance. So that was the problem with that. But you know what, if you want, sometime I can go through everything you're talking about, but the short answer is that everyone needs to be unique. No one needs any particular kind of religion. Everyone needs to see God the way they see their own God, but they should never limit themselves. My only point is that whatever you think of God, do not limit it. When you think of yourself, don't limit yourself, because you are God, and everything is endless. The bowl is not endless. This is the bottom of it, this is the top of it, this is the height of it. You are greater than this bowl, that's all I'm saying. This bowl has a limitation, therefore you cannot be this bowl, because you're endless, and this is not.

JAMSHID: You don't understand. What I'm saying is that the problem with the system is the belief that God is out there somewhere. We make this bowl, this God, big, based on our environment and traditions and societies. If you come into my country and say you're going to eat dog, they'd kill you. You have to leave the country. But you go to Korea or China, they eat dog. Everything we believe in now is based on our environment, our society, what we've been told. And we're told that God is this thing, but we don't know what it is. It's out there. Just pray to it, and you will get there. And I believe you will get there, I know for a fact you will get there. But bring it down a little closer. Take the control out of your surface experience and put it back into the program you have within you. What you are doing, Morrie, is transferring the control in your life, your internal program, and putting it into the hands of the Creator. This outside thing. All I'm saying is you should put it into the hands of the Creator inside you.

MORRIE: Let me ask you, what's your purpose of writing this book?

JAMSHID: I have one major purpose. I believe I am not what I think I am. I'm what the environment thinks I am. This book is a way of reflecting me to the outside world, how I want the outside world to see me.

MORRIE: What is your intention?

JAMSHID: My intention is to just reflect myself to the outside world.

MORRIE: No, that was your purpose. Why do you want the outside to know what you think?

JAMSHID: Because if everybody believed as I believe, there should be absolutely no war. There should not be killing or wanting. People do so much damage because of that single word, "Want. I want to have." They hide behind religion and create armies to attack and kill people. You see it in the news every day. I want this book out there to have an effect, for the same reason that Moses and Jesus and Muhammad came and brought their beliefs to lead people in a certain direction. They had an impact on society. I'm hoping I can have an impact on society. If people understand how insignificant they are, we could begin. If you could look at us like a bunch of ants, with lines on the freeways and traffic officers and rules, definitely you're going to laugh.

DAVE: I think I know where he's is going with this. Jamshid is not transcending "wanting" all the time. He's not in Step 7 all the time. But he's been there, and he wants to show us how to get there.

JAMSHID: Yeah. Eventually when you get there, it becomes a mission to share this. Nature forces you to share this.

MORRIE: That's the beauty of it.

JAMSHID: Yes, and I hope I can send a message, because I see it clearly. It's very difficult to put it on paper, but I can see the purpose clearly.

MORRIE: If there was one sentence you could put on your gravestone that would summarize your whole life, what would that be?

JAMSHID: I will never die.

MORRIE: No, but you die. Let's say you died.

JAMSHID: That's the message. I don't believe in death.

JAMES: That's what he should put on his tombstone. "I don't believe in death."

JAMSHID: I don't. You convert to something else. I'm not this bag of bones and flesh, I'm something else. I don't die.

MORRIE: And if you wanted to write one thing to say what your life was all about up to that point, what would it be? That your life was about what?

JAMSHID: An experience full of experiences. Interesting.

DAVE: What would you put on yours, Morrie?

MORRIE: That I made a difference, and I was a bridge.

JAMSHID: I think everybody in this world, at the end of the day, is doing something like this. In order to correct the environment, you start from here, inside. You can try to start from outside, but there's too much talking and not enough being. When you start inside, eventually you're going to change your environment.

DAVE: I think what Morrie said, being a bridge and making a difference, I think we'd all agree with that. What Bob does for a living, searching for the keys in DNA, what James is doing with the rainforests and the animals, and what you're doing with this book. I'd like to close by asking if any of you see anything in Jamshid's concepts, as stated in his book, that screams out, "Oh, that's wrong."

JAMES: It has to scream?

DAVE: It could mumble or mutter.

BOB: We talked about the word "death" and the connotations of that. It could bear some additional thought, maybe a different word. ["Oneness" was chosen as a better word for the seventh step.] But I understand what you're saying. Death is a state of mind. And when our carbon-based life form ceases, we don't cease. Because we are not who we look like. We are who we are inside. We are part of and one with the universe.

JAMSHID: Yes.

BOB: That is big. I understand that. I understand the concept. It's not completely at odds with science, and I think science can support some of it, and we can rationalize some of it, but we don't have the tools to rationalize and quantitate all of it.

DAVE: Or to dispute it?

BOB: Or to dispute it. Right. So concepts of faith, and some of the things you said, are superb. We don't, in the science arena, ever have debates like this. They don't. I mean, the Human Genome Project had to put aside $10 million to force scientists to hold meetings to think about things like ethics and theology, because we don't do that. It's not something we do. To answer your question, no, I don't see any disconnect here with anything that I know, and, for anything that I am or the world that I exist in, it can be in harmony.

DAVE: How about you, James?

JAMES: No, nothing screams. And because, as we sit here today, you haven't finished the book, I don't know exactly where you're going, but I'm not sure it's a step-wise process, that you need discrete steps and can't just sort of burst through someplace. So I don't think it's as clean as the 7 Steps you presented. We have a thing like regression and the service of the ego. Suppose you're at Step 7 and suddenly something happens. Where do you go back to? Do you go back to 1? Or 4? What about balance? But from what I've seen, no, I don't have major problems with this.

DAVE: And Morrie gets the last word.

MORRIE: If I may say one concept and one comment. The concept is that you shouldn't be thinking about everything there is to think about, and if you think about everything, don't say everything that comes to your mind. And if you say everything, don't put everything that you say on paper. I think it's going to be a great process. They asked Michelangelo, "How do you get such a beautiful sculpture out of an ordinary piece of stone?" And he says, "I just remove the extra pieces."

BOB: It was in there the whole time.

MORRIE: Yes. So I think you have great concepts, great pieces of stone to sculpt. I was working on a book for five years and finally stopped because I kept changing and changing it and got so tired of it. So finally I had to put it aside. Balance being the center of this – I love it. Because life is all about balance. In Kabbalah, one of the 10 steps is *Tiferet*. That means beauty, and beauty is balance. The universe is balance. So to have balance as the center of your 7 Steps, it's so good. At the end, we travel from being separate to being one. Oneness. Everything comes to be one thing. Jamshid is your name, and Morrie is my name, and at the end, these are just what separate us. When you go deep into it, you're not Jamshid and I'm not Morrie. We're one, OK? So that's when you get to the very end of it. That's a perfect system. So I hope that your book will become a perfect system that can bring order is this world of chaos that we live in.

Epilogue

Suppose, then, that all men were sick or deranged, save one or two of them who were healthy and of right mind. It would then be the latter two who would be thought to be sick and deranged, and the former not.

Aristotle

Putting the thoughts of a lifelong journey onto paper has been an education in itself. Much of the mindset of the 7 Steps to Wisdom and Inner Peace is nebulous, by necessity. Forcing these ideas into black-and-white proved an enjoyable challenge.

At the end of this book, you begin your own journey. That's what it's all about. Every word of this book is about you, not me. It's meant to serve as your road map.

You should be able to see the destination now.

As Aristotle suggested, the closer you get to wisdom and inner peace, the crazier you will appear to others. You won't be marching to their drummer anymore.

Don't let it bother you.

Don't let anything bother you.

Namaste.

Works Cited

Armstrong, Karen. *A History of God*. New York: Ballantine, 1993.

Atmore, Anthony, et al. *The Last Two Million Years*. London: The Reader's Digest Association, 1973.

Barbour, Ian G. *Issues in Science and Religion.* New York: Harper Torchbooks, 1966.

Beveridge, W.I.B. *The Art of Scientific Investigation*. New York: Vintage Books, 1950, 1953, 1957.

Buscaglia, Leo F. *Personhood: The Art of Being Fully Human*. New York: Ballantine Books, 1986.

Byrne, Rhonda. *The Secret*. New York: Artia Books, 2006.

Capra, Fritjof. *The Tao of Physics: An Exploration of the Parallels Between Modern Physics and Eastern Mysticism*. Berkeley: Shambhala, 1975.

de Riencourt, Amaury. *The Eye of Shiva: Eastern Mysticism and Science*. New York: William Morrow, 1980.

Ferris, Timothy. *The Whole Shebang: A State-of-the-Universe(s) Report*. New York: Simon & Schuster, 1997.

Finley, Guy. *The Secret of Letting Go*. St. Paul, Minnesota: Llewellyn, 1996.

Fromm, Erich. *The Art of Loving*. New York: Harper & Row, 1956.

Gardner, Dr. James. *Jesus Who? Myth Vs. Reality in the Search for the Historical Jesus.* Bangor, Maine: Booklocker, 2006.

Hawking, Stephen. *A Brief History of Time: The Updated and Expanded Tenth Anniversary Edition.* New York: Bantam Books, 1998.

Hick, John. *An Interpretation of Religion: Human Responses to the Transcendent.* New Haven: Yale, 1989.

Jones, Judy, and Wilson, William. *An Incomplete Education.* New York: Ballantine Books, 1987.

LeShan, Lawrence. *The Medium, the Mystic, and the Physicist: Toward a General Theory of the Paranormal.* New York: Ballantine Books, 1969, 1973, 1974.

Lovejoy, Arthur. *The Great Chain of Being: The Study of the History of an Idea.* New York: Harper & Row, 1960.

Ming-Dao, Deng. *365 Tao.* San Francisco: Harper-Collins, 1992.

Needleman, Joseph. *A Sense of the Cosmos: The Encounter of Modern Science and Ancient Truth.* Garden City, New York: Doubleday, 1975.

Ornstein, Robert E. *The Psychology of Consciousness, second edition.* New York: Harcourt, Brace, Jovanovich, 1977. First edition published in 1972.

Perkins, James S. *A Geometry of Space-Consciousness, second edition.* Adyar, Madras: Theosophical Publishing House, 1973.

Polson, Beth. *Secret Santa.* New York: Atria, 2003.

Prabhupada, Swami A.C. Bhaktivedanta. *Bhagavad-Gita As It*

Is. Vaduz, Lichtenstein: The Bhaktivedanta Book Trust, 1983.

Sagan, Carl. *Cosmos.* New York: Random House, 1980.

Saltzman, Paul. *The Beatles in Rishikesh.* New York: Penguin Studio, 2000.

Siu, R.G.H. *The Tao of Science: An Essay on Western Knowledge and Eastern Wisdom.* Cambridge: M.I.T. Press, 1957.

Stenger, Victor J. *Physics and Psychics: The Search for a World Beyond the Senses.* Buffalo: Prometheus Books, 1990.

Taimni, I.K. *Science and Occultism.* Adyar, Madras, India: Theosophical Publishing House, 1974.

Talbot, Michael. *Mysticism and the New Physics.* New York: Bantam, 1981.

Westfall, Richard S. *Science and Religion in Seventeenth Century England.* New Haven: Yale University Press, 1958.

Zukav, Gary. *The Dancing Wu Li Masters: An Overview of the New Physics.* New York: William Morrow, 1979.

Internet Resources:

Astrobiology: The Living Universe. ThinkQuest Team. http://library.thinkquest.org, 2007.

Bulletin of the Atomic Scientists. http://www.thebulletin.org/doomsday_clock/timeline.htm, 2006.

Columbia Electronic Encyclopedia. http://columbia.thefreedictionary.com/Scientific+pantheism, 2006

Flat Earth Society. http://www.flat-earth.org/, 2006.

Gaia Theory. www.gaiatheory.org, 2007.

Gaia Theory: Science of the Living Earth. David Orrell. www.gaianet.fsbusiness.co.uk/gaiatheory.html, 2007.

Hinduism. http://www.indhistory.com/hinduism.html, 2006.

Mysticism and the Idea of Freedom: A Libertarian View. Neal Donner. http://www.friesian.com/donner.htm, 2007

National and World Religion Statistics. http://www.adherents.com/, 2006.

Origin of Religion. http://www.allaboutreligion.org/origin-of-religion.htm, 2006.

The Patriarchs and the Origins of Judaism. http://www.jewfaq.org/origins.htm, 2006

Stanford Encyclopedia of Philosophy. http://plato.stanford.edu/entries/qt-entangle/1, 2007.

United Nations of Roma Victor UNRV History, Christian Persecution (online) http://www.unrv.com/culture/christian-persecution.php, 2006

Wikipedia. The Free Encyclopedia http://en.wikipedia.org, 2007.

Wilkinson Microwave Anisotropy Probe. http://map.gsfc.nasa.gov/m_uni/uni_101bbtest3.html, 2006

Television programs and feature film:

22ⁿᵈ Century. PBS science program. "World Wide Mind," Jan. 29, 2007.

60 Minutes. CBS News. "Bin Laden Expert Steps Forward." Nov. 14, 2004.

The Elegant Universe. NOVA. Science programming from PBS. (online) http://www.pbs.org/wgbh/nova/elegant/program.html, 2006.

What the (Bleep) Do We Know? A Film by William Arntz, Betsy Chasse and Mark Vicente, Lord of the Wind Films, LLC, 2004.

BOOKS

O is a symbol of the world, of oneness and unity. In different cultures it also means the "eye", symbolizing knowledge and insight. We aim to publish books that are accessible, constructive and that challenge accepted opinion, both that of academia and the "moral majority".

Our books are available in all good English language bookstores worldwide. If you don't see the book on the shelves ask the bookstore to order it for you, quoting the ISBN number and title. Alternatively you can order online (all major online retail sites carry our titles) or contact the distributor in the relevant country, listed on the copyright page.

See our website www.o-books.net for a full list of over 400 titles, growing by 100 a year.

And tune in to myspiritradio.com for our book review radio show, hosted by June-Elleni Laine, where you can listen to the authors discussing their books.

MySpiritRadio